THE SECRET TO TRUE AND LASTING HAPPINESS

BY

RANDALL F. GAGNE

the **Peppertree Press**
Sarasota, Florida

For information regarding permission,
call 941-922-2662 or contact us at our website:
www.peppertreepublishing.com or write to:
the Peppertree Press, LLC.
Attention: Publisher
1269 First Street, Suite 7
Sarasota, Florida 34236

ISBN: 978-1-61493-101-0

Library of Congress Number: 2012912650

Printed in the U.S.A.

Printed August 2012

DEDICATION

This book is dedicated to my children,
Sean, Ryan, Trevor and Patricia.
As your dad, there are many things
I can do for you in this life,
however, when it comes to your relationship
with your Heavenly Father,
I can only show you the door,
You, yourself, must walk through it.

ACKNOWLEDGMENTS

*I would like to thank wholeheartedly all members of
the Mitreya Center for Spiritual Studies in Bradenton,
Florida, for their invaluable contributions to this particular
philosophy. Over ten years of weekly meetings have
accumulated over one thousand hours of stimulating
spirited discussions about the nature of Truth.*

*Special thanks to Gopi and Neela Chari,
Irek Hicks and Craig Hancock.*

*I would also like to acknowledge Beth,
my wife of over thirty years.
She has modeled for me unconditional love
and real integrity. I love and respect her more
than anyone else on earth.*

*I also have to acknowledge my Lord and Savior,
Christ Jesus, without whom this book would
never have been written. I love Him with all my heart,
with all my mind, with all my strength and
with all my Soul. He is my Lord, my Master,
my Teacher, my Brother
and my best Friend.*

PREFACE

This is a true story. It is also a story about Truth. It is more or less autobiographical; however, the story is not about me, though I am sharing with you an extremely personal account of my life.

I'm just your average Joe who was lucky enough to stumble upon an extraordinary discovery, a treasure beyond imagination. Once I claimed it as my own, it transformed my life. It is this treasure I wish to share with you.

The Secret to True and Lasting Happiness is a treasure map of sorts. If you comprehend what is written within, you too can claim this treasure for yourself. In doing so, your life will also be transformed. Gone will be the days filled with pain and suffering, depression and anxiety. Those who claim for themselves the treasure hidden within will surely experience a constant stream of joy, even in the midst of drama and chaos. They will feel whole and complete and really, honestly, truly happy.

May God bless you in your search for true and lasting happiness.

Peace,
Randall Gagne

TABLE OF CONTENTS

INTRODUCTION

I was soaking in my Jacuzzi on a crisp December evening, enjoying the warm water and a view of the rising full moon. On the outside all was tranquil and quiet. On the inside, however, a storm was brewing. My mind reeled as I recalled the past year. It seemed as though every aspect of my life was unraveling. My wife no longer seemed interested in me. After fourteen years of marriage and three sons later, I couldn't really blame her. I was working myself to the bone and yet still going deeper and deeper into debt—not to mention, I had become fat, bald and boring.

With Christmas only two days away, combined with the fact that I hadn't finished my shopping yet, my stress levels were going through the roof. The truth was, I put it off because I *hated* Christmas shopping. I didn't really enjoy shopping at all, and Christmas shopping was a forced duty, so that made me very resentful. After all, I was still trying to pay for Christmas past and I knew with certainty that this Christmas was going to catapult me right into bankruptcy. I was barely making the minimum payments on our debt as it was. I felt I had no choice but to surrender to the inevitable. I just couldn't deprive my family of Christmas. They couldn't be happier. They love this season and I love my family.

I began to think about the current reality of my life. I was so unhappy. How did my life get so far off track? How could so much go so wrong so fast? Life was now a constant stream of frustration, anxiety and misfortune. I always seemed to be in the wrong place at the wrong time. Nothing went my way. If it could go wrong, it did, and at the worst possible moment—Murphy's Law. Why do I feel so unlucky? What did I do wrong? Why does it feel as if the Universe is constantly taking a dump on me? My mother's words echoed through my mind, "If you don't make your first million before you're forty, chances are you never will." My fortieth year was not far off, and I couldn't have been further from my goals. Not only was I nowhere near becoming a millionaire, I was quickly falling deeper and deeper into debt. A few years earlier, I had quit the family business. I couldn't afford to provide my family with the lifestyle to which they had become accustomed. I just couldn't work any harder. As a matter of fact, I was getting burned out. I didn't enjoy my work any more. What was I going to do?

In the mid 70s our family emigrated into the U.S. from Ontario, Canada. My father had invented a new manufacturing technique for applying vinyl onto paper. He patented it and was hired as a consultant by Imperial Wallcoverings, the largest manufacturer in the United States. In a short time, he had made enough money to move us all to Florida to start our own manufacturing facility. For twenty years we experienced tremendous growth and success. Before long, Gagne Wallcoverings was the largest manufacturer of textile wallcoverings in the country. I had a good paying job with benefits and a company car. I had the unique opportunity of working in every aspect of the business, from bookkeeping to manufacturing, to sales and marketing. I wanted to be a self-made millionaire like my father before me, so I worked very hard. My favorite aspect of the business was sales. I spent five years on the road establishing the Florida market.

I loved making cold calls and opening new accounts. For many months, my sales numbers in Florida were greater than the rest of the nation combined.

Looking back, I realized that I was not working so hard for my own success, but rather I was feverishly working to win my father's love and approval. However nothing seemed to impress him. I was starving for a few words of praise, a pat on the back, some recognition, something. Ever since I was a little boy, I idolized my dad. He was always there for us. He was our baseball coach in the summers and our ice hockey coach in the winters. There was nothing he couldn't build with his own two hands. When we were kids, he and I and my two brothers dug our own in-ground swimming pool. In the winter he would make us an ice skating rink in the backyard to practice hockey. He is very generous and well liked by all. He was always present and active in our lives, but at the same time, emotionally distant. I don't feel we ever really connected as friends. Currently, we rarely have intimate father and son talks. He doesn't like to express his feelings, and he rarely speaks about the past. This is torture for me, because I love him and want to be closer to him.

One day, about 20 years ago, I asked him why he didn't get more excited about the prospect of additional grandchildren. He told me that this only made him more anxious. Because he was the patriarch of the family business, he felt he was personally responsible for providing a good living for all. Additional family members just meant more mouths for him to feed. Because of these comments, I became convinced that I would never earn his respect as long as I was his employee, no matter how hard I worked or how much money I made for the company. I left the family business in an attempt to gain my own success and independence.

Through much practice and criticism, I had learned to become a master paperhanger, so I started my own company installing wallpaper. I did well, but not well enough to pay all our bills, keep my wife happy and raise three young boys.

As I soaked in the spa, reviewing my life, I had the realization that my impending bankruptcy would ensure a future devoid of my father's love and respect and this was too much for me to bear. I was soon overwhelmed with emotion and began to weep. It was a gut-wrenching, mournful, ugly cry. I never felt more alone, more lost. I had hit rock bottom. I was beginning to see quite clearly that my unhappiness was my own making. I had no one to blame but myself. I was responsible for every situation in my life because of the choices I had made. I became increasingly angry with myself. I called myself every name in the book for ruining my life, but I didn't know how to fix it. I had too much pride to go back to work for my parents or ask for their help. I couldn't stop crying. I was consumed with self-loathing and I just didn't want to be me anymore.

Out of sheer desperation I resorted to something I previously never considered. I decided to pray. If there was a God, I needed His help. But then I realized, I didn't know how to pray. I thought back to my childhood, when my parents had taken me to church. The Lord's Prayer! Yeah! That's what I'll do! Unfortunately, I could only remember the first two lines. I noticed the lights were still on in the bedroom, so I called to my wife, "Beth!"

"What?" she mumbled.

"Oops!" I thought. I think I woke her.

"What comes after, 'who art in heaven,' in the Lord's Prayer?"

"I don't know," she said. "I'm sleeping, come to bed!"

I tried desperately to remember, but I just couldn't. In utter frustration I broke down again. I turned my anger inward, scolding myself for being such an ignorant fool.

I then looked up into the night sky and pleaded, "God, please help me to at least remember my prayers!"

It was then that I felt a calming presence. I heard a very loud thought in my mind. **"For each line of the prayer, hold in your mind a mental image picture of whatever it means to you."** So, while I spoke aloud, **"Our Father who art in Heaven, hallowed be Thy name,"** I pictured in my mind an old bearded man sitting on a throne in the clouds.

While I held that picture in my mind, another loud thought popped into my head, **"Thy kingdom come, Thy work be done on earth as it is in heaven."**

"Yeah, that's it!" I thought. I repeated it aloud and pictured life-long enemies loving and caring for one another and soldiers putting down their weapons.

Again, a loud thought, **"Give us this day our daily bread."** I pictured in my mind all my needs and desires being fulfilled effortlessly. I saw myself having plenty of work and writing checks to pay off my debts.

Then again, even louder, **"And forgive us our trespasses, as we forgive those who trespass against us."**

It was at this point I questioned whether I was indeed remembering, or whether someone was actually communicating with me. It didn't matter, **"Focus!"** I thought of my parents, my brothers, my friends who betrayed or offended me and I forgave them. **"Deliver us from evil, for thine is the Kingdom, the power and glory, forever and ever. AMEN!"**

I had remembered the entire prayer. I began to feel my spirits lift as I recited it over and over. At one point I felt a strong urge to go under the water. So I sat on the bottom of the Jacuzzi in complete silence and solitude and recited the prayer in my mind along with the mental image picture show. Suddenly, I found myself talking to God effortlessly, as if I had been doing it my whole life. I thought, *This is so weird! I never really talked to God before tonight and here I am rambling on like some kind of seasoned evangelist.*

I wanted to know the meaning of life, so I asked God, "Why am I here? What am I supposed to do now? How do I find happiness? Are you out there? Do you hear me? Can you help me?"

With all the emotion and sincerity I could muster, I began to repeat over and over, "Dear God, please make yourself known to my heart and to my mind—I need to know that you are!"

Emotionally and physically exhausted, I drifted off to sleep. Two hours later, I was back in my body, still soaking in my spa, staring into a crystal-clear starry sky and a very bright full moon. I awoke with no memory of my dreams. I again started to pray, just as I had been before falling asleep. Please God, make yourself known to my heart and to my mind, I need to know that you are! I then thought to myself, *I'm going to drown out here in this Jacuzzi. I'd better get to bed.* I dried off and turned in.

I had the most peaceful sleep ever and awoke in the morning in an amazingly good mood. I was actually happy for a change. I was exceedingly happy.

It was Christmas Eve! I was so excited, I couldn't wait to go shopping to buy gifts for my family and friends. Wait a minute. I *what?* Don't I hate Christmas? Doesn't my wife call me a Bah-Humbug Scrooge? Don't I hate shopping? I thought to myself, *Well, not today apparently. That's weird, that's very weird.*

I don't recall exactly what I bought that year. However, I do recall that it was the most pleasant shopping experience of my life. I walked through the mall with a huge grin, humming along with the Christmas carols playing in the background, smiling brightly to all I passed, holding doors and wishing many a "Merry Christmas!" I even asked for assistance from the sales people, something I don't recall ever doing before. After finding just the right gift for everyone, I headed home.

Highway US 19 in Clearwater is a nightmare most days, but looked more like the mall parking lot on Christmas Eve. As I approached Drew Street, I noticed many police lights at the intersection. As I came closer, I could see that there was no accident. Instead the police were escorting hundreds of people though the intersection to an office building parking lot on the other side. In the lot I saw many TV news trucks putting up their satellites. Hundreds of people were standing in the parking lot staring and pointing to the windows of the building.

I was curious to know what was happening, however, I had to drive on. A few minutes later I heard a news bulletin on the radio. "A Christmas miracle has occurred in Clearwater, Florida! Thousands flock to an office building where a three-story image of the Virgin Mary has appeared on the glass on the front of an office building!" So that's what all the fuss is all about. A bunch of crazy religious fanatics worshiping a piece of glass.

"Fools!" I thought, as I laughed at their gullibility. How they could believe in God and miracles was beyond me. Up until this point of my life, I was an agnostic. I saw nothing in this world that would convince me that there existed a loving, omnipresent God. If He was ever present, why couldn't I perceive Him? If He was so loving, why doesn't He intercede when we are in danger? Why would He just stand by and watch us live lives of endless pain and suffering? If He was so forgiving, why are so many wracked with guilt? If He is so giving, why do so many suffer in poverty? If he is all powerful and all good, why is there evil in the world? There were just too many unanswered questions. It was easier to believe that those who believed in God were just superstitious fools.

Christmas came and went like most. The entire family got together at my parents' house. It was a typical Christmas, not unlike previous years; however, this year I was truly happy and at peace. All my problems felt as though they were a million miles away.

I spent most of the day relaxing on my deck and lounging in the Jacuzzi. I never felt better in my life. The difference in my mood and outlook was obvious, but I chalked it up to having a good cry. After all, it had been years and years since I cried. I never imagined it could make me feel this good!

While swaying gently in my hammock, enjoying the hot sun and cool breezes, I was startled by the sound of flapping wings directly over my head. I could feel the air being whisked across my scalp, so I braced for a landing. I opened my eyes just in time to see a beautifully colored pigeon land gently on the tip of the hammock stand. "Thanks a lot, bird. You just scared the hell out of me!"

I went back to my daydreams for a while, figuring he would fly away when he was ready. Minutes later my youngest son, Trevor, came out back. As he approached, he noticed the bird and suddenly became very still and quiet. Curious to see how close he could get, Trevor slowly walked toward the pigeon and reached out his hand. His eyes grew wide as he actually touched the bird and it didn't fly away!

I said, "Quick, Trevor! Go into the garage and get that old bird cage."

He returned in a few moments and to our amazement, I was able to just pick up the pigeon and put it into the cage! We took it in the house to check out our prize catch. I quickly noticed that it had red ankle tags with serial numbers. This was obviously someone's pet. It must have been a carrier pigeon. I did some research online and discovered that he was a Birmingham Roller.

He was really cool. He had personality. He would stick out his chest, walk in circles bobbing up and down going, "Buh ba boo, buh ba boo." Later that afternoon, I decided I would send my little buddy home to his owners. I took him out on the deck and let him fly away.

The next morning I grabbed some coffee and headed out to the Jacuzzi for my morning soak. As I opened the French doors, I was pleased and surprised to find that same pigeon waiting for me on the deck rafters. I brought him inside to show the rest of the family. We decided that since he returned on his own, he wanted to live with us. So we named him Fred and he became our new family pet.

A few days later I was befriended by a blue jay. Beth and I were in the spa when this baby blue jay hovered over us, squawking loudly. Beth figured he was hungry so I went inside and got a slice of bread. I rolled it up into small balls and the little guy gobbled them up. Every day thereafter, he would peck on the glass of the French doors leading into our bedroom. I would let him inside and give him bread and water. He would make himself at home and eat directly out of my hands. We named him Barney. Barney the blue jay, and Fred the pigeon.

One day while my parents were visiting, I noticed Barney on the fence. I said to my folks, "Hey, watch this!" I walked directly up to him, he ate out of my hands and then flew away. They were quite impressed as you can imagine. This went on for a while, until one day he grabbed one of Beth's gold rings off the table and flew out the door, up into the trees. We didn't invite him in any more after that, but I continued to feed him by hand when I was outside.

Later that evening as I lay soaking in my spa, I was overcome with the most intense feeling of Love. God, I love my spa and the deck that I built with my own two hands. I love my wife, I love my sons, I love my dog, I love my new pet birds, I love my home. I loved all these things, but I felt there was something else. I couldn't quite put my finger on it. Where is this intense love coming from? What else do I love? I love …I love …Jesus! And as I thought of the Lord, I experienced what I can best describe as swooning. I felt my head and shoulders relax backward and my chest heave forward. It felt as though a huge beam of love energy was exploding out of my chest. As I lay there basking in divine ecstasy, my mind began to analyze the current situation.

"Excuse me? Hello? What's wrong with this picture? You don't know Jesus, remember? You don't believe in God. How can you be in love with someone you don't know or believe in? This is not logical! How can I be distraught and depressed one day, and happy the next? Why am I so happy? I have no reason to be happier today than I was yesterday or the day before. What is going on?"

Even though my mind reeled with the obvious contradictions, my body didn't register them. I lay there experiencing wave upon wave of intensely beautiful emotions. I remember a deep sense of Peace that transcends words. I can only describe it as the complete and utter absence of fear. No doubts, no worry, no fear of any kind. No fear of abandonment or loss, no fear of illness or old age, or even death. I felt as though death could not touch me—that I would live forever. I just knew that the world and everything in it was perfect just as it was and everything was going to work out just fine. It was absolute bliss. Wave upon wave of Love, and then Peace, and finally Happiness.

I felt other emotions, which were foreign and unfamiliar, like Hope, Faith and Forgiveness. Not only did I feel forgiveness for all who had previously hurt me, I also felt forgiveness for myself, for all my weaknesses and poor choices. I *felt* forgiven. Until that moment, I had always believed that forgiveness was a verb, something we did. However at that moment, I was experiencing forgiveness as an emotion. My mind jumped back in. How can you feel forgiven when no one has forgiven you of anything? This is illogical! The disparity between my thoughts and my emotions was becoming more obvious to me. "What the hell is wrong with me?" I thought.

Then it hit me. "Oh my God, you've lost your friggin' mind!!" That was no ordinary cry. "You cried yourself right into a mental meltdown! You've created some alternate reality to escape your problems. Think about it. Overnight you fall in love with Jesus. You're no longer worried about your problems. You're exceedingly happy for no reason, you feel forgiven for no reason whatsoever, and you are no longer concerned about your impending bankruptcy."

"You poor bastard! I can't deal with this anymore," I thought. "I'm going to bed. **What time is it?** 11:11."

The next morning while drinking my coffee in the spa, I began to think about my future living in the loony bin. "Should I turn myself in or wait until they come and get me," I thought. "I can just hear the doctors giving instructions to the nurse, 'Give him 100cc's of Thorazine and put him in the padded cell!' Maybe this will all stop. Maybe if I keep quiet, nobody will notice."

Again my mind wandered back to the mental hospital. I saw myself mingling with the other inmates. I saw myself laying my hands upon them, praying for them, and healing them of their infirmities. Now I know I've lost my mind! Healing with my hands? Where did that come from? A thought like that has never crossed my mind before. As a matter of fact I've never heard of or seen anything like that in my life. "Oh, my God! What the hell is going on!? God, please help me! Please tell me what the hell is wrong with me. Why am I so freaking happy? Why am I in love with Jesus? Why are wild birds unafraid of me? Why do I think I can heal with my hands?"

Just then, a vivid memory began to surface from my subconscious. I was taken back to Christmas Eve. I saw myself praying feverishly to God to make Himself known to my heart and mind. The next moment, I see myself lying prostrate before Jesus. We engaged in a short telepathic conversation, and moments later I was back in the spa.

I leaped out of the hammock, Holy Christ!! No way! That's not possible! I can't take this. I need a beer. I went inside, grabbed a cold one and went to play with my boys.

Later that evening while I was soaking in my tub, Beth came out onto the deck in a bathrobe. "Can I join you?" she asked.

"Of course," I said.

She dropped her robe and slipped into the spa. Before I knew it, she was seducing me. "Wow!" I thought. "What is this? How nice. Where did this come from? Who cares!" My eyes rolled back in my head as I said to myself, "Thank you, Lord!"

We retired to the bedroom and as I made love to her, I started to feel guilty about feeling so incredibly good in my new reality when I knew she was still suffering. She carried the weight of the world on her shoulders, not to mention a chronic case of irritable bowel syndrome. Compassion welled up in my heart as I prayed for her.

"Dear Lord, please bless my beloved wife. She suffers so and I wish she could feel as wonderful as I do."

Immediately I heard a loud thought, **"So be it."**

"So be it? Really?" Another wave of intense love washed over me as we climaxed together. I told Beth I loved her and we passed out.

The next morning I couldn't stop thinking about all the weirdness in my life, even though my positive emotions and sense of well-being were still growing and expanding. How is it possible that each day gets better than the last? How is it that no negative thought registers fear in my body? How is it that no matter the torment of mental confusion, I still experience new heights of happiness and peace? How is it that my impending financial collapse has no effect upon me? Why am I so fearless? Why do I think I am capable of healing others with prayer?

Is it possible that my dream of Jesus was not a dream? It would explain a lot. *Are you kidding? Do you hear yourself? Do you think God actually revealed Himself to you?? It's far more likely that you've lost your friggin' mind.* Well, that does make more sense. I guess there are only two possibilities here. Either I've been blessed by God or I've lost my marbles.

Somehow I'm convinced that Beth is cured of her irritable bowel problems. When she comes home from work, I'll know for sure.

That evening I met my wife at the door. "Hi, dear, how was your day?" I asked.

"Pretty good and yours?" she replied.

"Fine. How do you feel?"

She had a curious look on her face as she said, "What do you mean?"

"How's your belly today?"

"Well, now that you mention it, it hasn't bothered me all day. Why?" she asked.

"Just curious," I said with a smile. *Well, so far so good,* I thought.

Later that evening after we put the boys to bed, I went for a soak in the spa. My mind reeled, as I tried to fathom the possibility that I had actually conversed with a guy who's supposed to have been dead for two thousand years. It makes no sense, I thought. Who the hell am I? I'm not religious. I don't go to church. I've never read the Bible. I don't know anything about religion or spirituality. I've lived the last thirty-six years of my life without believing in Christ or God. I've always felt those Jesus freaks were the most obnoxious people alive. Why on earth would Jesus pick *me*?

I wanted to escape from the confusion, so I went under water and sat on the bottom of the spa again. I enjoyed the intense stillness. I tried clearing my mind, but I was distracted by a sound. It was the sound of approaching footsteps. Normally, the sound of someone walking on the deck reverberates like thunder under the water. These footsteps were very subtle.

"Someone is trying to sneak up on me," I thought. It must be my youngest son, Trevor—only a five year old could walk so gently. I decided to play along. I was going to scare him before he could get me, so when I was sure that he was right next to the spa, I leaped out from under the water, raised my arms like an angry bear and let out a loud growl. To my astonishment and disbelief, there was nobody standing there. What the hell? I leaped out of the tub and ran around the back of the deck. There was no one there!

Now I was getting freaked out. I slipped back into the spa. It was chilly out there. I went under the water up to my eyeballs. I looked back and forth, extremely paranoid. I was sure I heard footsteps!

Just then, like before, I heard footsteps again, but this time they were walking away from the spa! My ears could here them, but my eyes could see absolutely nothing. Chills reverberated down my spine—I was completely creeped out. I grabbed my towel and ran into the bedroom, locking the door behind me. I peered through the French door windows, scanning the deck.

The next day, I had to return to work. My friend, Larry, had been working with me for several months. He was not just an employee—we were close friends. His wife went to high school with my wife. We hung out at the beach almost every weekend. I felt comfortable enough to share some of my recent experiences with him.

"Gee, I don't know," says Larry. "I don't know what to think or what to tell you. Are you going to church on Sunday, instead of coming to the beach?"

"I don't know," I said, "I really hadn't thought about it."

"I would think that the first thing you would want to do is go to church. Don't you?"

"That makes sense, Larry. However I just haven't been guided to go. I'll give it some thought though."

The next morning, I awoke feeling utterly reborn. No negative thoughts or emotions came to me. I gathered my coffee and whistled a tune on my way to work. On this day I was chattier than usual, and spent time getting to know my customers. As it turned out, this client knew my father. As I was leaving for the day, he said to me, "Tell your father that our mutual friend, Rolly, is not doing very well. He has really bad diabetes and he's had an open wound on his big toe that shows no sign of healing. He is scheduled for amputation surgery next week." He pointed his finger across the street and said, "He lives right there."

After packing up my equipment and just before driving away, I heard a very loud thought. **"Go to him, he needs you."**

Oh, Christ, you've got to be kidding! I thought. *I can't go knock on somebody's door I don't even know! What would I say?*

"GO!!"

"All right, all right!" I hesitantly approached the front door and rang the bell.

"Hello, can I help you?" asked the gentleman who opened the door.

"Yes, hello, my name is Randy Gagne. I believe you know my father?"

"Oh yes, come on in!" he says, as though we were life-long friends.

"My name is Rolland Temple, but my friends call me Rolly."

"Well, Rolly, I was working next door and heard that you know my father and that you weren't feeling too well."

"Oh, yes," he says while pointing down to his foot. "I've got this lousy blister that broke from playing too much golf and it just won't heal." I noticed that his left leg was purple from the knee down.

"My diabetes means poor circulation, so unfortunately my doctor doesn't think it will ever heal."

"Are you getting any kind of therapy?" I asked. "I know some massage techniques that may increase the circulation."

"A massage? Sure, why not!"

He lay on the couch and I started rubbing his shoulders and back. In only a few moments, he had drifted off to sleep. I knelt down by his foot and cupped my hands over the bandaged toe. I closed my eyes and went within. I began to pray. As I did my hands began to tremble violently. An intense vibration seemed to pulse through my whole body. In only a few minutes, my clothes were drenched and I was dripping sweat from my brow. I collapsed exhausted on the floor.

I glanced around to see Rolly's wife, looking in my direction with a very strange look on her face. "Are you OK?" she asked. "Would you like some coffee or something?"

Coffee sounded like the perfect thing I needed, so I nodded in appreciation. We chatted for fifteen minutes or so, until I noticed Rolly rising from his slumber. He came running out to the pool area to join us.

"Look at my foot!" he blurted out. "That's amazing! Look at the veins in the top of my foot, they're throbbing with blood! Look at my leg! It's the same color now as my good leg! How did you do that?" he asked, with a smile that beamed from his face.

"I don't know," I said. "It's a gift."

"Sure the hell is!" he cried. "Thank you my friend!"

I didn't know what to say, so I excused myself and headed home.

That was bizarre! I thought to myself. *What just happened? What the hell do I know about massage? Where did that come from? I don't think I can handle this.* I went home and mentioned nothing to my wife about Rolly Temple. Rolly

Temple. Sounds like Scooby-Doo trying to say Holy Temple. Rorry Tempo. Too weird!

While driving home, a mile or so from my house, my attention was drawn to a sign placed in the front yard of a home. The sign was an advertisement for aura photographs. They were very colorful and eye-catching. A very loud thought echoed through my mind, **"Go there for confirmation of your experience."**

Confirmation? I thought. *What kind of confirmation?* Curiosity got the best of me, so after dinner I went back to that house. It was not like me to knock on a stranger's door after dark, but I couldn't wait. I climbed up the front porch and rang the doorbell. A short, pudgy blonde woman about my age opened the door a few inches.

"Can I help you?" she asked.

"Yes," I replied, "I would like to get a picture of my aura."

"I don't have any film right now, so you'll have to make an appointment and come back next week."

"OK," I said and turned to walk away.

"Did you have a specific question for me?" she asked.

"No, I just wanted to see what my aura looks like."

"You have a magnificent aura," she said.

"Excuse me?"

"It's beautiful!"

"You can see my aura without the camera?" I asked with an obvious tone of disbelief.

"Yes, it was a gift I was born with. For a long time I thought everyone could see what I saw. When I realized this wasn't the case, I got into aura photography, so I had confirmation of what I was seeing."

"Yeah, right," I grumbled as I turned to walk away.

"You're marked!" she blurted out.

"Marked? What do you mean, marked?" I said as I whipped back around.

"I can see flaming emblems in your aura just over your head."

"Excuse me?"

"I can see a sideways figure eight, and a yod just next to that."

"A yod?" I said, "What the heck's a yod?"

"Well, it looks like a flame, and it represents the hand, so it probably means that quite recently you were touched by the hand of God."

Immediately I felt the sensation akin to ice cold water being poured over my head. The mother of all chills rippled down my spine, sending my entire body into convulsions. I turned around and tried to shake them off like a wet dog.

In the next breath she said, "And you're a healer!"

Once again, shivers consumed my body.

"Stop!" I said. "I can't take any more. I'm going home!"

I turned quickly and ran down the porch steps toward my car.

I drove home and spent the rest of the evening in shock, trying to comprehend the reality of my situation. I can't deal with this, I thought. No one is going to believe me. What do I do now?

I spent the next day frantically trying to find a dictionary that could shed light on this Yod thingamajig. Unfortunately, it was nowhere to be found. *That chick is crazy,* I thought. *There is no such thing as a yod.*

"**What time is it?**" Let's see, it's 11:11. I retreated to my spa only to drift back into an unshakable sense of peace and tranquility. I've never felt this good in my entire life. With each passing day, I achieved new heights of bliss. I'm thinking, there's no way tomorrow can be better than today. I was wrong.

The next day when I got out of bed, I don't think my feet actually ever touched the floor. I just floated about the house, humming and smiling. I made some coffee, and took my new best friend, Fred, out for a soak. As we walked out onto the deck, he flew off my shoulder and up into the rafters. A few minutes later, he flew down and joined me on the edge of the spa. He soon discovered a two-foot square area built for drinks, which was covered with maybe two inches of water. He jumped right in and started to splash about, getting himself soaking wet. He then spread his feathers apart and preened himself with his beak. When he did this, he looked like a fur ball, straight out of the dryer.

I was enjoying this immensely, when I noticed a squirrel jump out of the trees onto the far edge of the roof line. He ran all the way over towards us, leaped onto a rafter and climbed out until he was directly over our heads. Then he strained to get his head as far down as possible, and with a wide-eyed stare, gawked with a look of disbelief at this pigeon bathing with a human! I couldn't contain myself, so I burst out laughing. All I saw was a flash of fur and feathers, as they both scurried for their lives.

On the television was continuous coverage of the Virgin Mary story across town. Thousands of people gathered there to pray. They also erected a huge shrine in front of the glass image with thousands of flowers, candles and gifts. The tenants could no longer work in the building. Maybe these people aren't so deluded after all.

Is it possible that I've been the one spending my entire life living an illusion? I was convinced there was no God. I lived my life as if there were no God. Everyone in my life lived the same way. My whole world is being turned upside down. Oh, my God, is it possible that those Jesus freaks were right? What do I do now? I can't even think of anyone to talk to about this. No one I know talks about God. Well, I suppose the first thing I should do is go to church.

A loud thought popped into my head. **"No."**

"No? I shouldn't go to church?"

"No, not yet."

"How else am I going to learn?"

"I will be your guide to truth."

Oh great! Now I'm talking to myself!

As disconcerting as this was, I couldn't stop asking myself questions. And the strangest part was, I immediately got an answer to every question, and those answers made sense to me. How can I answer my own questions so quickly?

This is so weird! I was straining to come to grips with a new reality. Did I actually speak to Jesus? How could I? Didn't he die like two thousand years ago? It's not possible! Where did Jesus come from anyway? I didn't pray to Jesus. I just prayed to God. Is Jesus God? Did God send Jesus? Or did God reveal himself in a form I could understand? It seemed to be the only logical explanation for the bizarre events unfolding in my life. Why me? I'm not religious. I've never believed in Jesus. I don't go to church. I don't read the Bible. I'm certainly no saint. WHY ME?

I had no choice but to accept this new reality regardless of how unlikely or unbelievable. I could not disregard the intense feelings of Love and Peace that permeated my entire being. I felt saved and lost all at the same time. What do I do now? Where do I turn? Who can I talk to? Do I dare speak of this? I decided that at the very least, I needed to confide in my wife.

Later that night, I asked Beth. "How are you feeling today?"

"I feel great," she replied. "I haven't had any bathroom emergencies for days."

"You're welcome," I said, sitting there with a Cheshire cat grin on my face.

"What do you mean, you're welcome?" she said, with a puzzled look.

"I prayed for you to feel better and you do. So, you're welcome."

She just sat there looking at me with one eyebrow propped up.

"Honey, do you believe in Jesus?" I asked.

"Well, I'd like to. But I have my doubts, you know?"

"Yeah, I felt the same way, until I met Him the other night in the Jacuzzi."

Her head remained motionless, but her eyes widened and turned to lock on mine. "Excuse me?"

I told her of the bizarre events of the previous week. The dream of Jesus, the footsteps on the deck, the trip to Rolland Temple's house, the scary aura picture lady and the intense emotions of Love and Peace that were engulfing my body. She sat there and listened, but said nothing. She didn't know what to say.

Eventually she piped up, "That's lovely dear, but perhaps it would be best if you didn't mention this to anyone else, okay?"

She got up to leave, and glanced back at me with a look I'd never seen from her before. However, it did remind me of the look on Larry's face after I told him. It was the look of fear. As she left the room, my head dropped in despair, as I was beginning to see just how difficult this path was going to be.

What time is it? Hmm, let's see, it's 11:11."

That night I dreamed I could fly. Not like Superman or anything—more like an aging pelican, lumbering and clumsy. I flapped my arms to attain a height of ten or twelve feet, and then floated down again. Up and down. It felt as if the air were the consistency of water, like swimming up from the bottom of a pool. I remembered my dreams immediately upon awakening the next morning. Flying was the most fun I'd ever had in a dream. The flashbacks throughout the day kept a smile on my face.

Later that evening, I got a call from my mother. She told me she received a phone call from the Temples. They wanted her to tell me that when Rolland went in for his amputation surgery, they removed his bandages to discover a considerable amount of healing had occurred, so they canceled the operation. My mother wanted to know how I knew them and why I stopped by their house. I was as vague as I could be. I was definitely not prepared to discuss this with my mother.

Oh, my God! I thought, maybe I'm not crazy after all. Something is definitely going on here, and I need to figure out what it is. I need to go back and talk to that aura lady. I retreated to my tub to once again drift off into a sea of Love, bask in the light of His Peace and ride the intense waves of other emotions, like hope, faith and forgiveness. All was well in my world. I felt like a newborn babe with an entire lifetime of possibilities in front of me. I felt as if death couldn't touch me. I felt loved and protected. I had not a worry in the world, for every cell in my body knew my Heavenly Father loved me and would take care of me. I never imagined a person could ever be this happy.

This is way beyond happy. Words like happy, joy, bliss and ecstasy don't even come close to describing this indescribable sensation. The Peace is so great that no thought of fear can enter my mind or body. Each day I achieve new heights of bliss. Each day I say to myself, there's no possible way I can feel better tomorrow than I do today, and every day I'm proved wrong.

It was New Year's Eve day. I noticed my neighbor Mark, playing basketball by himself in his driveway. Over the course of the last year, he and I spent many hours playing ball together. We got along very well. On this day, however, I could sense there was something wrong. He just wasn't himself. He usually has a big smile on his face.

"What's wrong, buddy?" I asked.

"It's my little girl. She is very sick. I took her to the doctor the other day and was told she had a little bronchitis. The doctor said that I shouldn't worry, but she is out cold with a high fever and hasn't spoken a word in two days. She doesn't look good. I'm not sure what I should do."

He took me into the house and sure enough, his daughter was passed out on the couch. Her entire face was flushed red.

I said to Mark, "Why don't you let me try something? Maybe I can help."

"What can *you* do?" he asked.

"It's something that works for my kids, so let me give it a try."

I knelt down next to the couch and placed my hands on the bottom of her tiny feet. I went within and prayed for her silently. I felt a rush of heat surge through my body. I could literally see the color quickly returning to her tiny face. She batted her eyes a little and then peeped, "Hi, Daddy."

I moved up next to her and placed her limp hand in mine. I told her, "As you feel my hands getting warmer, you'll start to feel cooler, okay?"

She smiled and nodded.

Within a minute or two she sat up and said, "Daddy, I'm hungry."

She walked into the kitchen, sat down and ate an entire bowl of macaroni and cheese. When she finished, she climbed down and started to play with her dolls, happy as a lark.

I knew from that all too familiar expression on Mark's face that no explanation was going to suffice. He had just witnessed something he couldn't explain rationally. And Mark was not a spiritual person, he was a used car salesman. He couldn't handle it and freaked out. He asked me to leave and that was the last I heard from him. He and his family moved away shortly thereafter.

This sucks, I thought. I'm just trying to help. My friends are dropping like flies. Why are they so afraid of me? I wish they could feel what I feel. It was time to face that scary aura lady. I needed to talk to someone who knows about this stuff.

I went back and knocked on her door. The same woman came to the door.

"Hi, my name is Randy. I came by here the other night."

"Oh, yes. Hello, my name is Reverend Marcie. Would you like to come in?"

"Sure," I said. We entered and sat on bar stools next to the kitchen counter. "Did you say Reverend?"

"Yes, I am an ordained minister with a metaphysical church. I am also a Reiki Master," she said.

"A what?"

"A Reiki Master. I teach people how to heal with their hands."

"You're kidding!"

"Let me show you," she said.

She got up, went behind me and placed both her hands flat on my back. Immediately I could feel warmth emanating from her hands. And then very quickly, they actually got hot enough to freak me out a little.

"How do you get your hands so hot?" I asked. A part of me wanted desperately to know more and another part wanted to run out the door.

"Reiki is an ancient hands-on healing technique used by Jesus and Buddha. It was rediscovered by a Japanese doctor in the eighteen hundreds. I currently teach classes in it. All of my students are women, but in your case, if you're interested, you can come by and check it out."

"And people think this is normal behavior?"

"That depends on who you ask. My father is a traditional Baptist minister, and he doesn't accept it at all. In fact, he rarely speaks to me," she said as her mood became somber.

"I've never heard of anything like this until recently." I told her of my healing experiences with the Temples and my neighbor's little girl.

"I told you!" she cried. I could tell by the unique colors in your aura. She pulled out several of her pictures and explained what some of the different colors represented.

"Speaking of auras, I tried to find yod in the dictionary and I couldn't."

"That's because you were looking in an English dictionary. Yod is the tenth letter of the *Hebrew* alphabet."

"Well, what does it mean?"

"It's the first letter in the name of God, has a numerical value of ten, and symbolizes the hand."

"Why is it over my head? What does that mean?"

"I don't know. I've never seen one before."

I thanked her for her help and headed home. On the way I began to experience a new emotion. This one wasn't very pleasant. For the first time in my life, I felt ignorant.

Not stupid, like I had been labeled by my family since child-hood—just ignorant. I didn't know *anything* about God, Jesus, religion or spirituality. Why would Jesus reveal himself to such an ignorant soul?

This emotion continued to well up within me until I was nauseous. Right there and then I dedicated myself to a future of study, never wanting to experience this horrible emotion again. Only then did it subside and disappear. For the first time in my life, I *wanted* to read, to study, and to understand what was going on in the world. Surely someone has had an experience similar to mine. Someone must be able to shed light on what's happening. There must be a book out there somewhere to explain what was going on with me.

When I got home, I dug through a box of books, and found a dusty Bible in perfect condition. I propped myself up in the bed and opened to the first chapter in Genesis. I had only read the better part of the first page when a loud thought echoed through my mind.

""Only read the words in red."

In red? What words in red? I started flipping pages, but no red words. Finally, all the way in the back, I found words typed in red ink.

Matthew Chapter 4, verse 4, "Man does not live on bread alone but on every word that comes from the mouth of God."

That's so beautiful, I thought. I don't know what it means, but it feels good. I was captivated, completely absorbed in every word.

I then came to a passage entitled, "Jesus heals the sick." Heals? I was very pleasantly surprised to read how Jesus healed many through touch and prayer. My dreams and healing experiences were starting to make more sense. I guess this healing with the hands is not such a foreign concept after all. I did offer to work for Him. I guess healing is what he wants me to do. It gave me great comfort to think that any one who believes in Jesus and reads the Bible will accept what I do without freaking out.

After an hour or so, I was getting tired. Perhaps I should turn in.

"What time is it? 11:11." Instantly I had the strangest feeling of déjà-vu. It finally donned on me that practically every time I look at the clock, it's 11:11. That's so bizarre. Why on earth would I keep looking at the clock at the same time? Is there something special about that particular time? Or is it just the numbers? I decided to do a little experiment. I reset the clock ten minutes fast. Sure enough the next morning the first time I glanced at the clock it was 11:11. I got goose bumps on my arms. This is getting weirder by the day! I continued to see 11:11 each day, for weeks, months and years. It continues to this day.

Later that afternoon I was cleaning my bedroom. That may not rock your boat, but it got my wife's attention. She didn't fail to notice that I was reading the Bible and cleaning the house. She also noticed that I discarded my pornography, and that I was making every effort not to cuss. It's not that strange, is it? It wasn't outrageous behavior, but it was new.

I was experiencing firsts on a daily basis. Everything seemed new and interesting. I was like a sponge soaking in all life had to offer like a new-born babe. I viewed the world around me with new eyes. There was so much love welling up inside me I could barely contain it.

While I was cleaning, I heard my little Trevor coming my way screaming and crying. He came limping into my room, blood streaming down his shin. With his mouth agape and big alligator tears pouring down his face, he pointed down to a big scab on his knee he had just reopened. I felt so bad for him, immediately I could feel my hands getting hot. I knelt down and cupped my hands over the open wound. Within seconds, his sobs turned into a giggle.

"That tickles, Daddy!" A smile emerging from his face. A minute later he said the pain was all gone and he went about his way.

This is so cool! I thought. *I'm going to save myself a fortune in doctor bills!*

I spent the next few weeks working around the house, playing with my boys, attending Reiki healing classes and reading the Bible. I lived in a perpetual state of joy. No negative thoughts or emotions entered my body. Nothing dramatic or negative happened to my family or to any of my friends. Life seemed perfect. I knew my Father in heaven loved me, and was watching over me and that's all that mattered.

Then one gorgeous afternoon in early February, tragedy struck. The boys and I took Fred out for some fresh air and exercise. He would fly circles around the neighborhood a few times and then land on me. He'd never land in a tree, ever. He always flew directly back to me.

This day, however, shortly after my oldest son, Sean, let him loose, a huge hawk swooped down from out of nowhere and started to chase Fred. Sean, Ryan and I were standing in the driveway screaming," Fly, Fred, fly!!" Within a few seconds both had flown out of sight. The boys ran into the house sobbing. I just sat there dumbfounded. I waited and waited, but my pigeon didn't return. Why did this happen? I was devastated. I loved my bird. Why did God allow this to happen?

This was the first bad thing to happen in weeks and weeks. I counted back on the calendar. I had forty days of unending Peace. Well, like they say, all good things must come to an end. I didn't realize just how much Fred had worked himself into my family's hearts as well. News quickly spread throughout the neighborhood about the loss in our family. A few expressed their condolences.

Three days later, while Sean and I were feeding some baby ducks from the pond in the back, I noticed our neighbor, Kim, who lives down the street, driving towards us very slowly. Sean looked over towards her approaching vehicle and screamed, "Fred!!"

He ran down the driveway to retrieve his little buddy who was perched on the front of her car like a hood ornament.

"I was hoping that was the bird you lost!" she said.

"Where did you find him?" I asked.

"Yesterday I heard a noise in my garage. I could hear something flapping about in the vent behind the dryer. So I had my husband unhook the dryer from the wall and this morning, I found this bird sitting on my car. I thought he would fly away when I backed out of the garage, but he didn't. He just stayed on my car and kept glaring up in the sky, looking rather paranoid."

I laughed and said, "I guess so. I don't know if you heard, but he was chased into that vent by a hungry hawk!"

"I'm so happy you have your bird back. See you later!" she said smiling as she drove off. Fred was very happy to be home, and we were just as happy to have him home. We never really expected to see him ever again. He was terribly traumatized by the experience, and from that day forward, he never flew outside again. He would still go outside on my shoulder, but always with one eye ever-peering into the sky above.

That night I learned from Rev. Marcie that it was against the law to place your hands on someone unless you are a minister or a licensed massage therapist. She told me it would take about a year of classes, and she could ordain me into her church, or I could spend six months training to be a massage therapist. She told me of a massage school locally that had a very spiritual teacher.

The next day I went to Clearwater to visit the Bhakti Academe of Intuitive Massage and Healing. The headmaster, Dale, was a big guy like me, with a kind smile, not the least bit intimidating. He spoke very slowly in a deep whisper. I liked him. I liked the space. It felt comfortable and inviting. It felt right. I could sense I was surrounded by like-minded people. I felt a sense of belonging that I had never known before. I borrowed some money and enrolled in the school.

Before long I came to know my classmates, and discovered that many of them had profound spiritual experiences as well. For instance, the teacher, Dale, told me that his wife awakened in the middle of the night only to witness orbs of light floating around her bedroom and emitting angelic music. The spheres went through his pillow and directly into his head. He said that for several months after that encounter, he could do very large number calculations in his head. Unfortunately, his wife was really shaken up by that experience and the resulting changes in her husband, so she left the marriage.

Dale had an interesting past. He used to do war crime investigations, became a registered nurse, then worked as a licensed clinical social worker, and finally a massage therapist and teacher. He is so easy to be around, and easy to talk to. Massage school felt less like school and more like group therapy. I have to admit that the six months learning about life and healing massage from Dale was the best six months of my life. Thanks, Dale!

While here among these people, I also got over the question of, "Why Me?" I began to realize that people were waking up by the thousands all over the world. This wasn't about me, per se. I was part of a global movement, the awakening of humanity.

I also became good friends with many of my classmates. Two in particular stand out. They were two older Jewish women, Louise and Maya. They taught me a great deal about their faith and the Jewish religion. Maya especially was very devout, spiritual and religious. She was active in her temple, and invited me there for a special ceremony where she got to stand up before everyone and read from the Holy Torah. As I understand it, that is a rare thing to witness.

She also told me of an incredible mystical experience she had. She awoke in the middle of the night to use the bathroom, and decided to get a drink from the kitchen. As she was on her way back to bed, she was turning the lights off with the wall switch, however, the room remained brightly lit. She moved from room to room attempting to turn off the lights, when she suddenly realized that every room she entered became illuminated by her own body. She was luminous! That freaked her out so much she ended up spending some time in a mental hospital.

Louise also confessed to me a mystical experience of her own. She told me that Jesus had spoken through her. I asked her how she knew it was Jesus. She said there was no question about it. The things that came out of her mouth were, "not the things any Jewish woman would ever say." Like me, she was a closet Jesus freak. She dared not share this experience with any of her family, for Jesus was a forbidden subject.

One day, Maya and I were at my house doing a massage exchange. I gave her a massage first and then she reciprocated.

After she had finished, she kneeled on the floor above my head to do some healing prayer. I was face down on the table as relaxed as anyone could be, when I was startled by Maya letting out a horrific gasp, followed by a frantic, "Are you all right!?"

"Of course, why wouldn't I be?" I responded sarcastically. I looked up to see Maya's face, fraught with fear and concern. She jumped up and left the room. I got dressed, went out on my deck, and there I found Maya prostrating herself repeatedly. She excused herself and left hurriedly without an explanation.

A couple of days later, I got a phone call from Louise. She wanted to get together to tell me something important. Apparently, Maya had confessed to her that she had a bizarre experience at my house. Maya wanted Louise to tell no one, but she felt compelled to tell me the truth. Louise told me that while Maya was kneeling and praying for me, Jesus magically appeared in the room and then proceeded to plunge a crystal into the back of my skull, then disappeared just as quickly. This is what precipitated her gasp. I mentioned to Louise that Maya then prostrated herself on my deck and she told me that that is something Jewish women never do. What did I know? All I knew is that my life was becoming increasingly strange and bizarre and Jesus seemed to be the catalyst behind it.

Now I ask you, seriously, if all these crazy things happened to you, what would you do? It was at this point that I became obsessed with finding out everything I could about this man, Jesus. I needed to know what was happening to me. I didn't know, because I was so damned ignorant. I hated not knowing. I hated being in the dark. I vowed to rid myself of ignorance. I was intensely motivated to read and study everything I could about religion, spirituality and God. I had set myself upon the path of knowledge and understanding. My spiritual education had begun.

I had no way of knowing, however, that true spiritual education doesn't come from books. It comes from life experience. And when God Himself decides to take you under His wing, and teach you Himself, you never know what's going to happen next. His curriculum involves drama—lots and lots of drama. He knows me better than I know myself. He knows my weaknesses and my strengths. His training reveals and develops character. But first, basic training. Initially, He had to push me to my limits to see what I was made of, to see if I had what it takes to eventually become an agent of God.

Up until this point in my life, I had never had an enemy. I was very friendly and neighborly. I liked people and they liked me. We lived on a cul-de-sac and we knew everyone on the street. There were plenty of children in the neighborhood for my kids to play with and our neighbors were very friendly as well. We loved our home and our neighbors. Then one day, we had new neighbors. They were bad asses, long-haired, tattooed and black-leather wearing Harley Davidson bikers. They were very loud and intimidating. I tried to be neighborly, however, before long these people grew to hate me and my family. They made our lives a living hell for the next two years. They constantly harassed and attacked me, my wife, my kids, my neighborhood friends and my friends at school. I'm not going to go into detail at this time, because that's a whole new book. Quite frankly, I still find it too painful to relive those experiences in order to write them down and share them with you. Perhaps my next book will detail this chapter of my life, and besides, I wanted this book to be entirely positive and inspirational.

Let me just say this. Life lessons are learned through interaction with other people. When we consciously enter the spiritual path, God brings people and events into our lives and sets the stage as it were for our growth and development. Just because we have an experience doesn't necessarily mean we will learn the intended lesson. Have you ever asked yourself, "Why is this happening to me again?" The same scenarios will continue to confront us in life until we learn that valuable lesson. We can run, but we cannot hide. If you have asked yourself that question, then try to consider what lesson you are supposed to learn from it and then next time, try to respond differently.

After we successfully battled against evil, we were relocated here to Sarasota, Florida. Life since then has been peaceful, productive, enlightening and joyful. I'm still doing massage and healing, and participate in study groups and spiritual events at the Mitreya Center.

I spent the next decade in an obsessive search for Truth and understanding, reading everything I could get my hands on. I looked into every spiritual philosophy looking for anything that resonated with my own spiritual experiences. I studied the spiritual philosophies of Christianity (synoptic gospels), esoteric Christianity (Gnosticism), esoteric Judaism (Kabala), Hinduism (Bavagad Gita), Buddhism (Damapada), Taoism (Tao Te Ching), theosophy, metaphysics, quantum physics, sacred geometry and ancient history (see the Bibliography.)

Many ask me if I still experience crazy synchronicity and healing miracles today, fifteen years later. I'm very happy that the answer is **YES**. For instance, just last Christmas I had an extraordinary experience.

Beth and I were watching the movie, *The Da Vinci Code*

on television. The scene was in the Louvre museum, where the protagonist Robert Langdon, a symbologist, and detective Sophie were trying to decode a message written on the museum floor by a murder victim, Sophie's grandfather. They had figured out that the numbers portion was the Fibonacci sequence. The text read, "P.S. Find Robert Langdon." The police thought Robert was the old man's killer because of it. Sophie had a different idea. She believed it was a message meant for her personally. The message was for her to find Robert Langdon, because the dead man, her grandfather, used to call her Princess Sophie as a child.

"In the movie, she says, 'P.S.'?"

Robert says, "Yeah, post script."

She says, "No, Princess Sophie."

Immediately, I heard a voice in my head say, as clear as day,

"No, Pistis Sophia!" and in my mind's eye, I could see a golden cross with P.S. inscribed in the center.

I turned to Beth and asked, "What's Pistis Sophia?"

She glanced at me with a puzzled look and says, "I don't know."

Pistis Sophia sounds so much like princess Sophie. What the hell is Pistis Sophia? I was intensely curious, so I went to the computer and Googled it. I was pretty shocked when it returned a hit. I first opened the Wikipedia site. I found out that Pistis Sophia is Greek for Faith and Wisdom. What freaked me out the most was that it was also the title of a book, and not just any book either. The *Pistis Sophia* is referred to as the Gnostic Bible, a first or second century text that contains the secret teachings of Jesus given to his disciples *after* the resurrection! This book essentially starts off where the Bible ends. In the last chapters of the synoptic gospels, Jesus is said to have resurrected and then revealed himself to His disciples and over five hundred others. The Bible says Jesus remained in His light body among His disciples for forty days before ascending to heaven. No mention is made however of the teachings he gave His disciples during this period. This is where the *Pistis Sophia* comes in. According to the Gnostics, Jesus remained on earth for eleven years after His resurrection before ascending. This book catalogues His teachings during that period.

I asked my son, Trevor, to get me that book for Christmas. It was a difficult read, but I cherished it nonetheless. Because of it, I have a better understanding of Jesus, the nature of the cosmos, the ego, and the path of ascension available to all of us. It was at this point that all insecurities I had about the voice in my head as possibly being my own concoction flew out the window. I knew beyond a shadow of a doubt that I was in communion with the Lord. So much so, that I am willing to put it in writing and share it with the world. God is Real. God Is here now. We are all His children and He loves us unconditionally.

I am writing this book for those who have never before spoken to God. Have you ever had someone give you the silent treatment? Have you ever had someone you love pretend you don't exist, and completely ignore you? Doesn't feel good, does it? Please don't do this to your Heavenly Father. He is always around, always available to you, wanting to help. However, He can't help you if you don't acknowledge Him and ask Him for help. He gave us all the gift of free will. We can choose to have a relationship with Him or not, it's entirely up to us. God wants to be a part of our lives, but He is willing to wait until you are ready to come to Him. Go ahead, try it. All you stand to lose are your illusions. Love, Forgiveness and Truth are yours for the asking. The Lord is eager to reunite with His lost sheep. Simply go within your own mind and make a sincere plea to the Lord to reveal Himself to you. But be forewarned, once you do this your life will never be the same.

CHAPTER 1

GOD

The philosophy presented in this book is a collection of my own beliefs. I live my life by the truths presented within. The content for the most part is wisdom I acquired through life experience, my relationship with God, and many years of reading and participating in study groups.

I began to see the common threads of Truth woven through the tapestry that is the world's religions. All philosophers throughout history wrote about Universal Truths. The Lord Himself is the author of Truth. Man simply writes about how he perceives these Truths, telling his own stories, in his own words. This is what I have attempted to do here.

Why did I bother to write a book about my own personal philosophy? I'm sharing it with you because I am genuinely, honestly, truly happy. I have trials and tribulations like everyone else; however, even amidst the drama of life, the background emotion for me is happiness. For years prior to my awakening experience, I suffered from depression. Since that time, I have experienced no depression whatsoever, regardless of what's happening in my life. I've been sad, angry, upset and confused, but never depressed. To know God is to know Happiness!

The metaphors in Chapter 1 sprang from my own creative imagination. It is my attempt at painting a portrait of God with words. I'm simply describing what He is to me.

The remaining chapters for the most part contain wisdom gleaned from reading the books listed at the end in the Bibliography. There are, however, two exceptions. The first is the *service body*, found in Chapter 12, which is a concept coined by my good friend, Gopi Chari. He and I started the Mitreya Center for Spiritual Studies in Bradenton, Florida, many years ago. He is the most sincere seeker of Truth I have ever had the privilege of knowing. He and his wife, Neela, manifest blessings and miracles on a regular basis. They have helped me to grow on my spiritual path more than anyone else. They are perfect role models for anyone wanting to walk the Path to spiritual wisdom. Thank you, Gopi and Neela!!

The other exception is the *Karmic Quotient* found in Chapter 8. This is revelatory wisdom given to me by Jesus in a dream state. In an incredibly vivid dream, I was in a classroom setting, Jesus was the teacher and the subject was Karma. When I awoke, I immediately put pen to paper to rewrite my notes. This was the one and only time I've ever had such a dream, and the only time I have ever written down the contents of a dream. I've included it in this book because I consider it Truth and it is part of my philosophy of life.

I leave it to the reader to accept or reject any portion of this philosophy, as I believe everyone is entitled to believe whatever they choose.

In the spring of 2011 my son, Ryan, was struggling with addiction to prescription pain killers and checked himself into a rehab facility in south Florida. While I was visiting him, I became overwhelmed with compassion for those I met there and before I knew it, I was in the front office volunteering to give an oral presentation to the group. During the long drive home, I came up with the outline for this book. In an effort to compact all my knowledge and understanding into the shortest possible phrase, I came up with, "God is here now." It occurred to me that this phrase has twelve letters, and those in rehab were being taught the Twelve Step program. It seemed to fit perfectly. As soon as I got home, I set pen to paper to organize my thoughts. Nine months later, the pen stopped and before me was this book. The twelve chapters in the *Secret to True and Lasting Happiness* are an alliteration of:

GOD IS HERE NOW

God
Omnipresence
Duality

Illusion
Surrender

Happiness
Ego
Rules
Evolution

Now
Observer
Work

God is like some very ancient texts, untranslatable,
unspeakable, and unknowable.

God is like quantum mechanics,
mysterious and unfathomable.

God is like the starry heavens in the night sky,
infinite, boundless, eternal, awesome!

God is like fishing on a small lake in the early hours of
the morning, Serenity, Quietude, Stillness.

God is like a golden mean spiral,
Infinitely big and infinitely small.

God is like a child's imagination,
creative and unbounded.

God is like the word ineffable,
too Holy to be described with words.

God is like Jesus' healing ministry,
a source of miracles.

God is like a miracle,
mysterious and awe inspiring.

God is like Love,
The source of true Happiness.

God is like the whole universe,
Incomprehensible and indescribably beautiful.

God is like the world's oceans,
deep, vast, mysterious and unknown.

God is like the Grand Canyon,
awe-inspiringly beautiful,
overwhelmingly deep and vast.

God is like our sun, the source of all light and Life,
showing us the Way.

God is like space, we live within it,
move through it, it's everywhere and yet
it goes completely unnoticed.

God is like the oath taken in court,
the Truth, the whole truth,
and nothing but the Truth.

God is like a child's face on Christmas morning,
full of Hope, Faith and Joy.

God is like our breath,
functioning on an unconscious level,
synonymous with life itself, and ever present.

God is like being in Love, blind to all things negative,
unending happiness.

God is like the mother of all anti-anxiety medications,
making us feel invulnerable, indestructible and fearless.

God is like the mother of all entheogens,
making us feel intimately linked to the whole of Creation.

God is like the present moment, here now.

God is like Love,
inspiring selfless service to others.

God is like the raging hormones of a teenager,
likely to inspire self-improvement.

God is like Disney World,
the happiest place on earth!

God is like the mother of all antidepressants,
making us feel Happy, Joyful, Blissful, Ecstatic.

God is like an MRI,
allowing us to see clearly what is within us.

God is like a yearly employee evaluation,
Allowing us to see the parts of us
that need improvement.

God is like evolution,
pushing us towards perfection.

God is like the ultimate goal of Verizon Wireless,
Omnipresent coverage, can you hear me now?

God is like Miracle Grow for plants,
Helping us to grow up.

God is like the invisible man,
He sees you, but you can't see Him.

God is like a woman's womb,
the source of life, and resides within.

God is like having a GPS in our vehicle,
guiding us back to the right Path
after we have lost our way.

God is like a bountiful crop close to harvest,
filling us with Hope, providing us nourishment.

God is like a good dog, offering unconditional love,
even if you are selfish, obnoxious and ugly.

God is like a good cat,
content to wait for you to come to him.

God is like Jiminy Cricket, the voice of our conscience.

God is like the memory of our parents' admonitions
a voice in our minds urging us to be good.

God is like a light bulb going on over our heads,
the source of inspiration.

God Is like a sixth sense, the source of intuition.

God is like a close encounter with a UFO,
apt to change your view of Reality.

God is like a good hunting dog,
fiercely loyal, desiring to serve you well,
offering unconditional Love.

God is like having a relationship with someone
on the other side of a mirror,
you feel their presence, hear their words,
but you see only yourself.

God is like having a futuristic Google application
downloaded directly into our minds,
instant access to all knowledge.

God is like a child who listens intently
to his teacher and his preacher
He lives in His Holy abode, the present moment.

God is like Pi
infinite and indefinable.

God is like a master sculptor,
He simply removes what is unnecessary
to reveal what is already perfect.

God is like a master magician,
He uses illusions to entertain and educate.

God is like a good tour guide,
taking you where you want to go
and educating you along the way.

God is like a charismatic preacher,
inspiring us to do good.

God is like a master of meditation,
endless peace, peace, peace.

God is like a priest who takes confession,
forgiving everyone of everything.

God is like a restaurant owner
who has a vegetable garden,
He uses the best of the best for His own purposes.

God is like a priest who likes to play pranks,
He comforts the disturbed
and disturbs the comfortable.

God is like a good fireman,
He wants to save you from the flames.

God is like a good massage therapist,
offering a peaceful respite from the world.

God is like a good doctor,
a source of compassion and healing.

God is like a good teacher,
sees all, hears all, knows all.

God is like a good taxicab driver,
taking you on the right path,
and respecting your choice in whether
or not to engage Him.

God is like a good prophet,
a source of wisdom, healing and miracles.

God is like a good wife,
a close companion for life always there to go home to,
offering unconditional love.

God is like a good husband
anticipating and providing for daily needs
desiring to fulfill your wildest dreams.

God is like a good church
offering sanctuary, understanding and forgiveness.

God is like a good government
promoting equality, fairness and unity.

God is like the internet,
the connecting link that unifies all humanity.

God is like a hundred million dollars in the bank,
all the security you will ever need.

God is like any good parent,
He enjoys being recognized and appreciated.
and watching children display
humility, obedience and gratitude.

God Is like the absence of fear,
the Peace that surpasses human understanding.

God is like a genie in a bottle,
capable of fulfilling any desire.

God is like hangin' ten—totally awesome dude!

God is like a good song, inspiring us to sing
and dance,rejoicing and celebrating life.

God is like a well-played instrument, a source of beauty
resonating with us at the deepest levels.

God is like Truth, steadfast, unchanging, eternal.

God is like the Red Cross
giving abundantly in selfless service to others.

God is like applied wisdom,
the path of right-use-ness.

God is like a circle, always around.

God is like a bride on her wedding day,
breathtakingly beautiful,
the epitome of Love and Happiness.

God is like a child who plays peek-a-boo
and hide-and-go seek, hidden and then revealed.

God is like witnessing childbirth,
indescribable Joy, awesome Grace.

God is like the journey around a Mobius strip,
infinity itself.

God is like the journey around a tube torus,
we get there by first going within.

God is like a trillion dollars,
you don't have to see it to know it exists.

God is like a blank canvas upon which the artist
paints his masterpiece,
His children are like the paints, once applied to the canvas,
they are fused together and made one forever.

God is like a movie screen and the light projector,
both are real, but all movement, action, and drama
perceived are illusory and unreal.

God is like a blank canvas and a pallet of paints,
both are real, but the image perceived within the masterpiece is illusory, unreal.

God is like a loving parent, giving abundantly,
loving unconditionally, forgiving everything.

God is like a loving father,
He wants his children to grow up to be just like Him.

God is like a rich and powerful father,
He loves his children so much,
He happily fulfills their every desire.

God is like a loving mother,
ready to offer tender love and forgiveness
to any of her children who ask for it.

God is like understanding parents,
they never punish their children in anger,
they correct their children's behavior with
patience, love, wisdom and guidance.

God is like an understanding father,
whose son is having a nightmare,
He gently awakens him by assuring him
of what is real and what is not real.

God is like a wise and loving father,
He sends his children to college,
He continues to provide for them,
He keeps an eye on them, but He gives them free will,
the ability to make their own choices,
He knows that His children must become
independent of Him before they can
become like Him.

God is like the father of the prodigal son,
eagerly awaiting His child's return

God is like a loving father patiently waiting for
His children to graduate college, return home,
and work in the family business.

CHAPTER 2

OMNIPRESENCE

OMNIPOTENT

Throughout sacred texts, there are three words used most often in describing the divine. The first is *Omnipotent*, meaning all powerful. God is viewed as the omnipotent creator of the universe. It must take extraordinary power to create the entire physical cosmos and everyone and everything within it, right? Tremendous power is somewhat intimidating is it not? Perhaps this is why so many fear God. Human history is replete with examples of people who attained greater and greater power by instilling more and more fear. We have learned to fear those with great power and we tend to avoid things we fear, which is why I suppose so many choose not to seek out God. This is completely understandable.

We have also been told that God can be angry, vengeful and wrathful. We have been told that God is our ultimate judge, and stands ready to punish us for our sins, ready to cast us into a burning lake of fire for eternal damnation. Is it any wonder, so many choose not to seek him out? Nobody wants to be judged, punished or condemned, right?

I believe with all my heart that God is none of these things. I also believe that these are the most damaging untruths perpetuated by man. To view God as vengeful, wrathful, punishing or judgmental is synonymous with creating God in our image and likeness. This is false thinking. We were made in His image and likeness, not the other way around. We are like Him in essence, He is not like us. As above, so below—not the other way around.

God is pure and perfect Love. His influence on us is always positive. He offers us only unconditional Love and Forgiveness. God our Father has never punished any of His children, ever! Also, He has never been angry or offended by any of His children, ever! He may be Omnipotent or all powerful, but He is also infinitely gentle, patient, loving and understanding. To experience God's presence is to experience immense Love, Peace, Happiness, Forgiveness, Hope and Faith. In His presence all fear vanishes. To know God is to know divine Peace, the Peace that surpasses all human understanding. God's presence is like the mother of all anti-anxiety medications. His Peace makes us feel invulnerable, indestructible and absolutely fearless.

I'm not sharing this with you in hopes that you will believe me. My hope is that you will seek to experience this for yourself, not just create a new belief. Experience the truth, don't just believe in it. Seek the Lord residing within you and you will find Him.

There is another false belief perpetuated by man that stands as a huge stumbling block to our future spiritual growth and evolution. We as a society have established limitations on God's unlimited power. We can accept that God is the creator of the Heavens and the Earth, however, we have somehow drawn a line when it comes to God's ability to communicate directly with His children. We are considered perfectly sane if we talk to God and engage in prayer, however, if we claim to hear God speaking back to us, we are labeled psychotic, schizophrenic, delusional or insane. This is not always the case. Certainly there are those who are mentally ill, however, the truth is, God is speaking to all of us, all the time. The problem is we just don't recognize certain thoughts and urgings as coming from Him. We incorrectly believe that every thought and impulse we have is born of our own minds. This is an untruth, an illusion that needs to be remedied. Again, I'm not suggesting you accept this as a new belief. Go within and ask God to reveal Himself, to reveal His word upon your mind. Hear His words, experience His presence, know God for yourself.

OMNISCIENT

The second word used most in describing the divine is *Omniscient* or all-knowing. God is infinite intelligence. He has witnessed and recorded every single event in the history of the cosmos. He is witnessing and recording everything happening right now, everywhere in the universe. Only He in His infinite wisdom knows exactly what will happen in the future. Imagine if we had access to all that information and wisdom. I believe we do! The divine omnipresent, all-knowing mind of God resides within each of us. We only need to tap into it as Edgar Cayce did. Tapping into the mind of God residing within us is like having a futuristic Google application downloaded directly into our brains. We too have instant access to all knowledge.

Don't take my word for it—experiment with it yourself. Pray to God for understanding. Ask Him a question you deeply desire to know the answer to. Then still your mind as in meditation and listen intently for the answer to be revealed to you. This is a prayer request that God is anxious to answer. If you want to experience an answered prayer, ask for understanding. If we want Him to, He will reveal to us the Truth. What Truth? The Truth! The Truth of His Omnipresence. The Truth that **GOD IS HERE NOW**.

It's important that we not limit God's infinite knowledge and power and in the infinite ways in which He can reveal Himself to us. For example, He can speak to us through our family and friends or even a passing stranger for that matter. He can guide us to read certain books that may contain the Truth that we seek. He can reveal the Truth through strange coincidence or synchronicity. He can reveal His Truth to us in our dreams and sometimes, He simply brings to mind old memories. The following is an example of the latter.

A few years ago, my son, Ryan, asked me to give his girlfriend a massage. She had to stay home from work because of a painful, debilitating backache. Ever since Ryan was a little boy he would come to me any time he had pain. He has experienced healings many times himself, so he was quick to recommend me. And it was an appropriate request, considering the fact that I am a licensed massage therapist. Ryan and Alyssa were high school sweethearts, we adore her and she was like a part of our family. I told him to bring her to the house and I would be happy to give her a massage. I was just setting up the table in the living room when she arrived. I had every intention of giving her a massage, except I was feeling a strong inner urge to give her some Reiki healing instead. She guided my hands to her pain and we both began to relax. I started to breathe deeply and go within to tap into the Omnipresent mind of God, the source of all healing. I was focusing on clearing my mind, but I was distracted by a recurring memory. It was the memory of a patient I had treated at the rehabilitation clinic earlier in the week. She was a very attractive blonde who insisted on sharing with me her drama about having to spend days in the hospital with an extremely painful kidney infection. I chastised myself for reminiscing about a beautiful woman and went back to the task of trying to completely clear my mind. Instead, I continued to relive the same memory sequence again and again until finally the light bulb was seemingly turned on over my head, and I had an Aha moment. I had just realized that my hands were resting directly over Alyssa's kidneys. I withdrew my hands and said to her, "Alyssa, I think Spirit is trying to tell me that you have a serious kidney infection and you need to go to the hospital." I gave her a blank check and insisted she go to the walk-in clinic down the street. As it turned out, the clinic confirmed her kidney infection and sent her directly to the hospital where she spent the next three days. She was understandably a little freaked out by my unexpected diagnosis, but that kind of stuff happens around me. If God needs to convey Truth to someone around me, He will use me for that purpose. If God wants to convey Truth to me by using someone around me, He does that too, for He resides in all people. The infinite, all-knowing mind of God resides within each of us.

My favorite form of communication with the divine is synchronicity. It makes life infinitely more interesting. I find that because of it, I pay more attention to the world around me. We experience synchronicity when we live in the present moment, the abode of God.

God reveals Himself to me every single day. Every day I experience the same strange recurring phenomenon. Every single day my awareness is made to focus on a set of numbers. The same numbers appear every single day without fail. At least once and sometimes many times a day, I see the number 1111.

At first I saw it practically every time I looked at a digital clock. Before long I was seeing it everywhere! Honestly, at the beginning it was quite disturbing, because the frequency of these sightings went well beyond coincidence. However, over the years I have come to view this daily experience as a nudge or a wink from my Heavenly Father. It's just another way for Him to continually remind me of His eternal presence.

When my wife received a promotion at work, we were required to relocate to Sarasota, Florida. After we had narrowed down the search for a neighborhood, we began looking for a house. Unfortunately, at that time, nothing was immediately available in that neighborhood. I went within and asked the indwelling Lord for His assistance. The next day we got a call from a realtor letting us know that a contract for a house under construction in that neighborhood had just fallen through and we were being given the opportunity to snatch it up. It was a brand new subdivision with few houses or street addresses. We were told that we could go look at it—it was located on site 11, lot 11. The builder's job number for this house was 1111. I knew instantly this house was meant for me. We purchased it just in time to pick the amenities and color scheme. The builder informed us that it would be ready for final inspection on 11/11, November 11th at 11 am.

A few years later, my daughter Patricia informed me that she was pregnant and due to have her baby around Nov. 20. I said, " How much do you want to bet you'll give birth on 11/11? Sure enough, my grandson, Michael, was born on 11/11. When he left the hospital, he went home to 1111 Handy Oaks Circle. Patricia made her best friend, Christina, his godmother and, funny enough, her birthday is 11/11.

Patricia's birthday is 3/17, which when these numbers are added together equals 11. Michaels father's birthday is 11/22, a factor of 11. My birthday is 2/22, also a factor of 11, and my middle son, Ryan's is 11/1. My oldest son Sean has his birthday on 2/18 a total of 11.

Lately I see it on license plate tags, those that are due to be renewed in November of 2011. One of the places where I practice massage has 1111 as the last four digits of the phone number. My employee number at the spa is 111. Sometimes I get a few items at the store and my total is $11.11 on the receipt, or I get $11.11 in change. I see it on billboards, street addresses and television ads. I see it everywhere! It's so ridiculous that eventually it becomes humorous.

One day I decided to Google 11:11. I was happily shocked to find a message board for people experiencing this very strange phenomenon. Most comments were that they were happy to find out that they were not alone in having this experience. Many were questioning their sanity, and this web site was a huge source of relief for those suffering from anxiety over this. However, everyone still wanted answers. Why is this happening? In the end, everyone must decide for themselves the meaning behind these daily experiences of synchronicity. Whatever its purpose, for me it is divine. For me, it's God. God is like a child who likes to play peek-a-boo and hide and go seek, hidden—then revealed.

God can also communicate with us through nature. While I was strolling through the woods on the nature trails near my house, I stopped to rest on a bench. I went within to connect with God. I told Him I was open to receive a message perhaps from someone passing by. I waited a while but I was alone. I was just getting ready to leave when I noticed that about ten to twelve feet away, strolling down the middle of the path was a huge grasshopper. Here in Florida, I think they are called cicadas. I had never seen one before this day. This guy was about four inches long.

I went within and asked, "Is this my messenger, Lord?" I said, "All right, if this is your messenger, then he will come over here and climb onto my foot."

The big guy continued to walk directly towards me until I shifted my weight a little. He apparently saw me and then corrected his course to go around me. When he got directly in front of me, about three feet away, he reared up as if being blocked by an unseen force. He then turned 90 degrees and headed straight for me. When he got directly beneath me, between my feet, he reared up again, turned 90 degrees and proceeded to climb up on my left foot! You can imagine my surprise!

Later when I shared this experience with my friend, Rena, she asked me, "So what was the message?" I replied that I felt it was another example of God's omnipresence. The fact that He can respond to our silent prayers in real time is quite a lesson.

"What about the grasshopper, does that mean anything to you?" she asked.

I thought for a moment, and I recalled one of my favorite television shows from my childhood, Kung Fu with David Caradine. In the show, he was a spiritual initiate, learning Kung Fu while living in a Shoalin monastery in China. His Kung Fu master was an old blind man who affectionately called him, "Grasshopper."

"Well, there you go, that's your message—you are the grasshopper."

"God's spiritual initiate!"

"Hey, yeah, cool!" I said.

OMNIPRESENT

The third word used most often to describe the divine is *Omnipresent*. This means that God's awareness is ever-present. It follows that for God to be all-knowing, he also has to be present everywhere. Nothing escapes His all-seeing eye. He witnesses everything everywhere at all times.

God's Omnipresence is like being under surveillance by the government. We are never really alone and everything we do and say is being recorded. I realize this sounds a bit creepy and possibly disturbing, but some Truths are downright scary. But Truth is Truth and we have to embrace it, whether we would prefer to or not.

In the lost gospel of Thomas, the author describes omnipresence much more eloquently. It reads, "The kingdom of heaven is within you and all around you, not to be found in buildings made of wood and stone, split a piece of wood and you will find me, lift a stone and I am there." If that is too abstract, perhaps a simpler more straight forward metaphor is easier to remember. God is like a circle, He's always around.

For me personally, this particular Truth was the very first I embraced. After all, it was the only way I could logically explain my experience of God. He answered my prayers in real time, while I was all alone in my spa in the wee hours of the morning. That could not have happened unless He was listening to my prayers as I spoke them. Logic dictated that either God was Omnipresent or I was psychotic. I didn't want to believe that I was mentally ill, however, I could not reject that as a possibility either. One of them had to be true. Either God had revealed Himself to me or I was insane.

God also has the power to communicate with us directly if he so chooses. I'm sure it doesn't happen very often as you can imagine. Most of the time, His words and guidance are so subtle that we mistake them for our own thoughts. He has no desire to send us into biological shock or cause us to question our own sanity. Can you imagine what it would be like to have God speak to you in a clear audible voice? I don't have to imagine it. It happened to me, just once. About seven years after my initial awakening, after many years of study, and after having witnessed many healing miracles, I had my most profound experience to date. I was in a particularly ebullient mood. It was a gorgeous day, so I decided to stretch out on the lounge chair on my porch and enjoy the cool breezes. It had been a long hot summer, so this cold front was a welcome change. I lay down and closed my eyes. I took a deep breath and let out a loud smile. I went within and began to speak to the Omnipresent Lord.

"Thank you, God, for this beautiful day! I am so happy. I love you so much! I love you with all my heart, with all my mind, with all my strength and with all my soul. I am your humble servant, now and for all eternity. I can't think of a greater life experience than being a vessel for your divine blessings. Thank you for being a part of my life. Thank you for saving me from myself. Thank you for filling my heart with your Love and Peace. Thank you for filling my mind with your Wisdom and Knowledge. Thank you for filling my hands with your healing energies. I am so very, very happy Father! I must admit, however, that I am still uncomfortable with the thought of sharing my experiences of You with others. Occasionally, I still hear a voice in my head that says, "You know Randy, you're really just insane, right? There is no God. You have created all this in your mind. Think about it. You asked for God to reveal Himself to your heart and mind because you needed to know that He existed. You fulfilled your own need. Almost every spiritual experience you've had has been entirely subjective. No one else feels what you feel. No one else hears what you hear. What have you seen, really? Nothing! You're delusional, insane!"

"Father, I hate having these doubts. I want to be able to tell others about you, but I can't. I'm afraid that that voice in my head is right. I need to know that I'm not insane. I need to know that you exist outside of me as well as within me. I need to see something phenomenal, something outside of myself, something I can see with my own two eyes, something that convinces me that You are omnipresent. This is very important to me Father, so I'm going to make this prayer every day until I do see something."

Immediately, the Lord responded to my prayer in a loud clear voice. I heard within my mind a deep, rich booming male voice that seemed to come from everywhere and nowhere. God said to me, **"Very well my son, open thine eyes and look to the sky."** I flung my eyes open widely and looked towards the small area of sky that was visible from where I was. I didn't dare move or blink for fear of missing something. The sky was bright blue with just a few scattered low hanging clouds. In my mind I'm thinking, *what am I possibly going to see in the sky that would convince me of God's existence?*

Within a few seconds, a small cotton-ball-like cloud floated slowly into view. It was so close, I felt I could reach up and touch it. It was the only thing in the sky. I kept an eye on it but continued to scan the remainder of the sky for a sign. Then I noticed that the cloud was breaking up as if caught in a jet stream. I continued scanning the sky but my eyes were drawn back to the cloud. I noticed that it now resembled a large number three. As I continued to gawk in amazement,

I realized that the cloud had reformed itself into a perfect Sanskrit AUM, oriented directly towards me. I could barely believe my eyes. As soon as I recognized it, my eyes flooded with tears. The cloud began to break apart as I buried my face in my hands and bawled my eyes out.

"Oh, my God, I can't believe you just did that for me. I am so blessed. Who am I, Lord, that you would perform such a miracle for me? Thank you, thank you! That was so perfect, exactly what I needed. You are so awesome! I'm sorry I doubted you, Lord. I will never ask for a sign again. You are indeed the Omnipresent Lord of the Universe. You are within and without. I exist within You, and You exist within me. I love you, Father. Thank you, thank you, thank you!!"

A few weeks earlier, the family and I had taken a short vacation in Orlando to go to Universal Studios. In the Marrakesh section, there was a shop that specialized in making custom brass pendants to be hung from a necklace. My son, Trevor, and I each got one. They had a menu of dozens of symbols from which to choose that were then engraved onto the pendant. I chose for one side the open hand with a spiral in the palm, which was the symbol for a spiritual healer. Since I was a massage therapist and Reiki healer, this seemed appropriate. For the other side, I ended up picking a Sanskrit Aum. I had never seen this before, however, the menu said the symbol represented the Word of God. I liked that and it also was very appropriate. I was wearing that pendant when God created the Aum cloud. That's what I call synchronicity! I later read about AUM in Paramahansa Yogananda's autobiography. He writes, "Patanjali speaks of God as the actual cosmic sound of AUM that is heard in meditation. AUM is the Creative Word, The whir of the Vibratory Motor, The witness of Divine Presence. Even the beginner in yoga may soon hear the wondrous sound of AUM. Through this blissful spiritual encouragement, he becomes convinced he is in communion with supernal realms. AUM of the Vedas became the sacred word HUM of the Tibetans, AMIN of the Muslims, and AMEN of the Egyptians, Greeks, Romans, Jews, and Christians. It's meaning in Hebrew is *sure, faithful.*"

I thought a great deal about this concept of Omnipresence. As a matter of fact, I couldn't stop thinking about it. The idea had deep ramifications. For one, it means that at no time have we ever been separate from God. So why is it that so many experience themselves as being separate from God? Obviously this in an illusion, and absolute impossibility. How is it that I could spend thirty-six years of my life in ignorance of his presence? At first it felt as if He had just entered my life, but upon reflection, I realized that He had only recently entered my awareness. He was always there in the silent background. This triggered another realization. He has always existed in the silent background of my mind, listening to my every thought. Yikes! That's another disturbing Truth. There is no such thing as a private thought! God is listening to and recording every thought, word and deed. I'm never really alone, even in my own mind. Logic then dictates that every thought we have is essentially prayer. Every desire we entertain is essentially prayer; therefore, spoken prayers are not absolutely necessary. Since thought precedes speech, God knows what we want before we ask for it.

It also occurred to me that if I am intimately linked to God and everyone else is also intimately linked to God, then I am linked to everyone else through God. This clearly explains certain unexplained phenomena like telepathy and clairvoyance. His indwelling, all-knowing, all-powerful mind explains experiences such as precognition, distance

Reiki healing and answered prayers.

My mind reeled as I pushed past the constraints of the finite, only to fall headlong into the deep end of infinity. Omnipresence, what is that? Infinite awareness, all-knowing intelligence pervading all of space, penetrating all matter, inhabiting every mind. God is like quantum mechanics, mysterious and unfathomable.

I tried to think of a real world comparison, a metaphor that the average finite mind could use to grasp a concept as abstract as omnipresence. It came to me one day while watching a Verizon Wireless commercial on TV. I'm sure most remember their "Can you hear me now?" campaign. No matter where we are, if we were to ask God that question, the answer would always be YES! There is no place we could travel to and be separate from God—even deep space. God is within us and all around us. He is the source of our very lives. He is the reason we have consciousness and intelligence. We are never separate from Him even in death, for death itself is another illusion. There is no death, only a shift in consciousness awareness. We shift from the illusion of separateness to the reality of Unity. But we don't have to wait for death to experience our connection, for God is available to us here and now. **GOD IS HERE NOW!**

Have you ever wondered how cellular devices work? Have you ever thought about the "empty" space surrounding us? These devices show us that space is not empty, but rather full of vast amounts of information. All cellular broadcasts, radio station broadcasts, and the internet can be accessed anywhere. They all exist in every cubic inch of space, just like God's all-knowing, ever-present mind. The internet with all its associated information is but a fraction of what is readily available to us naturally.

We each own a device capable of tapping into universal knowledge or the Omnipresent mind of God. That device is our brain. The brain is similar to a CB radio, capable of receiving and transmitting information. The medium for all that information is the invisible matrix upon which all matter is suspended, the all-encompassing ever-present mind of God or divine consciousness itself.

We have all always been intimately connected to our source. Unfortunately, however, that understanding remains for the most part an untapped potential. Anyone who studies the case of America's best known psychic, Edgar Cayce, should be convinced of these truths. There are over fourteen thousand documented psychic readings given by him over the course of his life, most of which were proven highly accurate. He himself came up with the term "Akashic records" when asked during a reading where he got his information. He described it a storehouse of information, the sum total of the consciousness of mankind. I'm sure sincere experimentation would convince any skeptic, for the omnipresent Lord of the universe exists within each of us, right here, right now, ready to bestow wisdom and knowledge to any who seeks it.

However, there is a right way to ask to achieve results. God is like any good parent, He enjoys being recognized and appreciated. He also enjoys watching His children display humility, obedience and gratitude. When our Heavenly Father returns our love, it is experienced as *intense happiness*. I invite you to experience this for yourself. Simply go within and start a silent conversation with the indwelling Lord. Talk to Him as you would your best friend. Ask Him, no beg Him to reveal Himself to you. Be prepared, however, for once He answers you, your life will never be the same.

According to the Bhakti Sutras, it is entirely our

responsibility at first to find God by surrendering our free will, but once we find Him, it then becomes His responsibility to continue to reveal Himself more fully.

Our new responsibilities now center around self-awareness, self-improvement and self-control. Our path through life is no longer our main concern. He will provide, He will guide, He will instruct and educate and He will reveal Truth. We are now tasked with recognizing and eliminating untruths and illusions. We need to recognize our true selves, our true natures, and our true source. This is the path that leads to true and lasting happiness here and now. How do we go about doing this? First we have to understand the nature of our earthly reality or duality consciousness.

CHAPTER 3

DUALITY

You probably recognize the word *Dual*. Not as in take ten paces, turn and fire duel, but rather like dual exhaust, meaning two-fold. Duality is a reality wherein all things have an opposite or dual nature. Duality pervades the entire physical universe. Everywhere in the physical cosmos, there is Goodness and evil, Light and darkness, Love and fear, Peace and conflict, Joy and sadness, Connectedness and separateness. Everything under the sun has an opposite or dual nature.

However, this is not the only reality. In God's spiritual kingdom, the place we go to after exiting our physical bodies, we experience only oneness or Unity Consciousness. Enlightened souls who live on earth also experience Unity Consciousness. Jesus referred to this when He said, "If thine eye be single, thy whole body shall be filled with light." *Thine eye* refers to our personal perspective on the world around us.

Do you perceive a world of opposites or do you see a world completely interconnected, one with the Omnipresent mind of God? With the latter, our perspective is singular, Oneness, Unity. Look past the drama of duality to the peaceful Oneness of Unity. In the Heavenly Spiritual Realms, duality does not exist. Unity reigns. In heaven there is only Love, Peace, Joy and Oneness.

The symbol that I feel best represents duality is the Chinese symbol Yin Yang. Two opposites brought together in balance and harmony into a single wholeness. The wholeness of balanced polarities is called Unity. This is the only true reality. It is Reality with a capital "R".

Duality is an artificial construct, a fabrication, an illusion, very similar to the holodeck in the *Star Trek* movies. Our earthly reality is similar to a 3-D fully interactive hologram. It only has the appearance and feel of reality. Duality is in essence Unity, distorted by perception. For example, if we were to hold up a single pencil in front of our face, and then cross our eyes slightly, we would then perceive two pencils. One is distorted into two. For duality to exist, we must first have Unity. For we cannot have two, without first having one. So they both exist within the same space and only appear to be separate. Thus the illusion.

An enlightened soul can exist here on earth in the physical plane, however, they can perceive oneness or connectedness in a world of seemingly separate things. Their reality includes only Love, only Peace, only Happiness. They are not fooled by illusions, because they can perceive Truth. Their eyes are uncrossed, as it were.

WHY DOES DUALITY EXIST?

If indeed the physical cosmos is an artificial construct and illusory, why did God create it? Why did He place us here in a world seemingly separate from Him? If He loves us, why are we made to suffer? It certainly feels as though

He is angry with us, doesn't it? Has He really cast us out of Heaven as some sort of punishment? The answer is NO! God is our Father and He loves us more than we could possibly imagine. We are not being punished, nor are we cast out of Heaven forever. There is a definite reason and purpose for us all being here on earth.

There is a beautiful Hermetic axiom that will help us to understand. It's, "As above, so below." This means that this world is merely a reflection of the eternal realm. We are a microcosm of the macrocosm. Truth is Truth, whether here or there. For us to better understand our Heavenly Father, we need to start by observing our best fathers here on earth.

On earth, a wise and loving father loves his children unconditionally. He provides for their daily needs and does his best to fulfill their desires within reason. He provides nourishment, comfort and security. He offers encouragement, understanding and forgiveness. He provides wisdom and guidance when necessary. There is nothing his children need that he does not happily provide. However, there comes a point in each child's life when they need to learn to stand on their own two feet and provide for themselves. So what does a father do? He sends his children off to college. There they learn how to live on their own. A good father does not abandon them altogether. He continues to provide their daily needs and He keeps an eye on them, but he gives them free will, the ability to make their own choices. He knows all too well that his children will make some very poor choices that will likely cause some pain and suffering, but then that is how we learn, is it not? After they have gained their independence and learned all the necessary lessons, they are welcomed back home.

In Heaven we as God's children lived in Paradise, having all of our needs and desires fulfilled. God is like any good father, He desires His children to grow up to be just like Him. There is one big problem however. It is impossible for His children to become like Him while they live in Paradise. Why? Because in Paradise, God gives abundantly, loves unconditionally and forgives everything. He gives and *we receive only.* There is no way for us to learn how to be giving, because every need there is met, there is no one to give to! We can't learn how to love unconditionally because while in paradise we all exist as pure consciousness. We are all equally perfect as He is perfect. It is easy to love those who are as equally perfect as we are, right? And how would we learn to be forgiving? Everyone in Paradise lives in a constant state of Peace, Love and Joy. Everyone is the same, no inequality. So what's to forgive?

God created the physical cosmos of which this Earth/ school is a part. A place where there is *seeming* inequality, imperfections and separateness. A place where we could learn how to be like our Heavenly Father by giving abundantly, loving unconditionally, and forgive everything. Earth is basically college for souls. While we are here, He continues to provide for our daily needs, He keeps an eye on us, but He also gives us free will, the ability to choose for ourselves. Because He is loving and fair, He established a set of universal laws designed to keep our world balanced, and to make sure everyone gets exactly what is due to them based on the choices they make. These laws are detailed in the chapter on Rules.

Once we learn all the appropriate lessons He would have us learn, we are welcomed back home into Paradise. How long this process takes is completely up to us. We are eternal beings after all. We can take as many earthly lifetimes as we need. We can sit back, enjoy the ride, and let our evolution unfold naturally or we can choose to work hard at returning home sooner rather than later. Free will—it's completely up to us.

If you find this difficult to believe, ask yourself this question. If earth is a prison and we are here to suffer punishment, why did God send us Jesus and the prophets? Does a jailer offer up the keys to freedom to those imprisoned? Of course not! The Truth is, God our Father loves us unconditionally. He is not angry with us, nor is He punishing us. He wants us to overcome, transcend this world of illusions and return home to Him. And He is ever ready and willing to offer us assistance to do just that. We need only to ask Him for it, but asking is a prerequisite. God loves us so much, He has given us the ultimate gift. The gift of free will. *He will NOT interfere in our lives until we ask Him to do so.* We must surrender our free will before He can offer His help and assistance.

How Do We Overcome Duality?

We can learn to overcome just about anything by simply bringing in awareness and understanding. Duality is no different. First we must recognize the fact that our objective reality in the world out there is one of opposites. Secondly we have to realize that duality also extends to our inner, subjective world as well. Duality is our very nature while incarnated in the physical world.

Overcoming this duality requires us to recognize our inherent two-fold nature. As human beings, we are all a combination of body and soul, physical animals with spiritual consciousness. We each possess a lower nature, an ego or personality and a higher spiritual nature or Soul. The word hu-man means angel man. Our Earthly expression is two-fold, part God and part man, or woman.

We must also become aware of the seeming dual nature of our minds. The mind is constantly being bombarded by opposing thoughts. It's like having an angel on one shoulder urging us to be good, and a little devil on the other tempting us to be bad. It is for this reason that most people are confused and really do not know what they want. It's the nature of this inherent inner conflict, which is the source of external conflicts. If we can gain a balanced mind, we have hope of attaining a balanced life. Our task is to learn the difference between the voice of our ego and the voice of our God-self or Soul within. We cannot serve two masters. We must choose which to follow. Most people choose to follow the urgings of their lower natures or egos. It is after all the loudest and most insistent of the two. To be on the Path, evolving spiritually, it is essential that we seek to follow only the urgings of our higher spiritual natures.

How do we learn to recognize the voice of God within us? Carlos Castaneda's teacher, don Juan Matus, taught him about our inherent duality and the egoic mind, but referred to it as a "foreign installation." In Carlos' *The Active Side of Infinity*, don Juan says, "…I repeat to you what I said before about our two minds. One is our true mind, the product of all our life experiences, the one that rarely speaks because it has been defeated and relegated to obscurity. The other, the mind we use daily for everything we do, is a *foreign installation*."

"Every one of us human beings has two minds. One is totally ours, and it is like a faint voice that always brings us order, directness, purpose. The other mind is a *foreign installation*. It brings us conflict, self-assertion, doubts, hopelessness."

" They found out that if they taxed the mind with inner silence, the foreign installation would flee … the foreign installation comes back, I assure you, but not as strong … Discipline taxes the foreign mind to no end," he replied. "So through their discipline [they] vanquish *the foreign installation*."

The "Pistis Sophia" teaches also about our dual nature. Jesus calls the higher nature soul and the lower nature the "counterfeiting spirit." It reads, "…They give the old soul a cup of forgetfulness, from the seed of wickedness, filled with all the various desires, and amnesia, and immediately, when the soul drinks from the cup, it forgets all the regions where it has been …And that cup of water of forgetfulness takes on form outside the soul, and it imitates the soul in all its forms and resembles it, and this is what is called the *counterfeiting spirit*."

" …and the *counterfeiting spirit* tempts the soul and continually forces it into all its lawless actions, all its passions and all its sin, and it holds steadfast to the soul and is antagonistic to it, forcing it to perform all this evil and all these sins. Now then, Mary, this is in fact the enemy of the soul, and this coerces it into all sins."

The voice of our ego always promotes selfishness, and the voice of our true selves would have us serve God and our fellow man. This test will never fail to help you distinguish between the two.

Have you ever caught yourself saying, "I knew I shouldn't have done that!?" God is like Jiminy Cricket from Pinocchio, He is the voice of our conscience or the inner urging we feel trying to stop us from doing something we know to be wrong. It's also like the memory of our parents' admonitions, urging us to "be good!" God is the still small voice within saying, "You know if you do that it's going to come back to bite you in the ass, right?" God is also the voice of inspiration, or intuition. Have you ever asked yourself, "How am I ever going to fix this?" just to have the perfect answer pop into your head? God's voice is very subtle, and is most of the time drowned out by the loud boisterous voice of the ego. We must learn to listen carefully for His wisdom and guidance. Again we cannot serve two masters. One path is wide, followed by many, and leads to endless pain and suffering. The other path is narrow and leads to Peace and Happiness— few find it and even fewer follow it.

After we have made the conscious choice to listen to and obey the voice of God within, then we are tasked with changing our perspective, our view of the world outside of us. Awareness and perception are universal inherent aspects of who we are. When we were babies born into this world, we already possessed awareness and perception. However, we could not cognize the world around us. We had to learn how to cognize this world of opposites, this reality we call Duality.

Now we are tasked with learning how to cognize or recognize Truth within a world of illusions. We have to learn how to perceive Unity within Duality or the connectedness of seemingly separate things. This process is synonymous with enlightenment itself. As Jesus said, "If thine eye be single, thy whole body will be filled with light." Thine eye being single means to be able to perceive Unity or Oneness, the inherent connectedness of everything in existence. It also means being able to perceive our connection to source. It means being able to see God in all people, places and things.

Overcoming duality requires us to adopt a new philosophy, a new personal paradigm. Eventually, things that at one time seemed very real and important, may become less real, less important. That which you previously perceived to be unreal or illusory may become for you more real, more important. It is a process that happens over time. The Path to God is like a father whose son is having a nightmare. He gently awakens him by assuring him of what is real and what is not. Our Heavenly Father is our guide to the world of the real. His Light of Truth shines in a world of darkness, showing us the Way. To find it, however, we must be searching for it, prepared and expecting to find it. We must be ready and willing to traverse it, believing in our hearts that it is the only path worth walking, the only path with real long-term benefits.

The first step in overcoming the illusion of duality, is to constantly ask ourselves this question: Who's to say what's good, and who's to say what's bad? This simple question will eventually help us to live a life without judgments. Why is this important? The difference between a life lived with judgment versus one lived with non-judgment is as dramatic a difference as journeying across the ocean in a canoe versus a cruise ship. When we judge everything under the stars as being either good or bad, right or wrong, fair or unfair, we then experience a constant flux of emotion. We are happy then sad, happy then sad, up and down, up and down, like a canoe riding up and down every single wave in the ocean. Living in non-judgment is like a cruise ship ride, balanced, calm, harmonious. Without judgments, there is no drama, no chaos, no fear. To embrace non-judgment is to embrace Peace.

We all know that words taken out of context can be very misleading. We also know that a still frame from a video recording can be equally misleading. Life itself is very fluid, always in motion and constantly changing. There is no possible way for us to perfectly predict how any single event will affect the future, right? If we are unable to see the future, how can we accurately judge what is happening today? We can't! Unless we're psychic, of course, which most of us are not. So, whatever may appear to us today as being good or bad, may in fact appear to us tomorrow as being the opposite. So of course, the wise thing for us to do is not to judge!

The following is a story about a wise old man and his horse. The story illustrates this point quite well.

There was once a wise old man, a rancher who was well-known, much liked and respected by his family and friends. He owned a beautiful black stallion, which had become his closest friend since the old man's wife had passed away. He entered his horse into a local fair. He was so beautiful and intelligent, he came in first place. The news traveled quickly and soon friends and family were stopping by the ranch to offer their congratulations. They would say something like, "We are so happy for you that your stallion won first place, isn't this exciting?" The wise old man would simply shrug his shoulders and quietly say, "Who's to say what's good and who's to say what's bad?"

The following week one of his ranch hands failed to lock the horse's stall correctly and during the night, the black stallion got out and ran away. Once again the news spread quickly and family and friends stopped by to express their condolences. They would say, "We are heartbroken by your recent loss, isn't this just terrible?" Again, without emotion the old man just shrugged his shoulders and said, "Who's to say what's good, and who's to say what's bad?"

A few days later to everyone's surprise and delight, the black stallion returned on its own, however, he was not alone. The black stallion walked back into his corral with three beautiful mares following right behind him. Friends and family returned once again and said, "Wow, this is fantastic! What tremendous luck you have. You must be terribly excited by this new development." But again, the wise old man just replied, "Who's to say what's good, and who's to say what's bad?"

The following week, the rancher's son was attempting to break in the mares for use on the ranch when he was thrown off and injured badly. He had to be taken to a hospital where he spent several weeks. Family and friends would stop by the hospital to wish him a speedy recovery. They would say to his father, "We feel so badly about this tragedy. You must be so upset about your son's bad fortune." The wise old man responded simply, "Who's to say what's good and who's to say what's bad?" No one could have predicted, however, that his son would fall madly in love with his nurse and take her for his bride.

A few months later after returning home with his new bride, there was a wicked thunderstorm. The thunder and lightning spooked the horses and several of them, including the black stallion, got out once again and ran away. The old man was out of town on business, so his son, knowing how much his father loved his horse, took every available ranch hand and went out into the storm to retrieve his prize stallion. While they were all away, a landslide buried the main house, destroying it completely. Very soon, everyone in the community showed up to see the damage done by the landslide. One by one they approached the wise old man to express their heartfelt condolences for his tragic loss. To each he would say the same thing.

"Please do not be saddened by recent current events. I know you feel very bad about what's happening to me right now, but I had learned long ago not to judge events in life, for there is no way for us to know what God has planned for us. I find it's best to just trust in His all knowing wisdom to have faith that He knows what's best for us. I believe everything that happens to us has reason and purpose and we should not judge God's purpose. However I choose to believe in His love for me, so I know that everything I experience day-to-day is designed to make me into a better man. You may choose to judge this carnage as a tragedy worthy of bad feelings, however, I choose instead to perceive the miracle. No one was killed in this natural disaster. My home can be replaced, my family cannot. I feel extremely blessed to still have my entire family in light of this event. I invite you to feel joy for me as I do, instead of feeling bad, for in the big picture, who's to say what's good and who's to say what's bad?"

His friends and neighbors were so moved by the wise old man that they all pitched in and together they rebuilt his home along with a second home for the old man's son, his new bride and old man's new grandchild. Who's to say what's good and who's to say what's bad?

The next step in overcoming the illusion of duality is to constantly remind ourselves to, "Just let it go!" Contrary to popular belief, the purpose of life is not to fulfill every selfish impulse whenever possible. We are by our very nature, here in the physical world, desirous beings. Our minds are bombarded by thoughts of personal desires. We want this, we want that, we want, want, want! And once we want it, we want it now! Every word we speak, every action we undertake is fueled by some personal desire. If thoughts were rockets, then desire would certainly be its fuel. The greater the intensity of emotion, the more likely our thoughts are made manifest. Emotions and desires are of themselves, neither good or bad, however, selfish desires of the ego cause suffering, and selfless desires of the soul cause happiness.

Upon closer examination, we will discover that most of our daily suffering is self-inflicted. Let's say that we have an intense desire for something and we set out to fulfill that desire. If we want something and can't acquire it, we suffer from *frustration*. If we want something and we're forced to wait for it, we suffer from *impatience*. If we want something and its no longer available, we suffer from *disappointment*. If we are made to wait too long we may suffer from *anger*. If we see someone else in possession of our hearts desire we suffer from *jealousy*. If we want something that is promised to us we suffer from *expectations*. If the person who promised it to us, runs off with it, we suffer from *betrayal* and *heartbreak*. If we come to believe that we will never have our desire fulfilled, then we suffer from *depression*. Now let's imagine that none of these happen. Let's say that instead we acquire our heart's desire. Once we acquire that which we desire, our happiness is short-lived and we then suffer from a nagging *fear* of loss. The possibility of losing it fills us with *anxiety*. We buy insurance and lockboxes in an attempt to avoid this suffering, but it's there nonetheless.

That's quite an emotional roller coaster ride for a simple desire, isn't it? Nonetheless, we all experience them on a regular basis. They are natural human emotions after all. However, we posses the ability to choose whether or not to engage in them. We do have a choice. We are practicing nonattachment and growing spiritually when we choose to remind ourselves to "just let it go!"

I had a good lesson on attachment early on in my massage career. A local chiropractor saw potential in me and offered me one of his unused offices to practice massage. He referred his clients to me and paid me a fair commission. I decorated the walls with my licenses and certifications and such. I loved my space, I loved my job, and I enjoyed immensely working with Dr. Bob. Then one day about three years later, he informed me that he was retiring and I had to vacate the premises. While I was packing up my stuff, I realized just how attached I had become to my office. I even shed a tear, which took me by surprise. I knew full well that it was not my office—after all I never even had to pay rent. I was using it for free, and yet somehow I came to think of it as mine. If I was this attached to something I knew wasn't mine, how much more attached am I to things I consider mine? From then on, whenever I occupied a new space, I would remind myself not to become attached to it, that I was there temporarily. Last year my boss at the spa asked all therapists to remove any personal items from our rooms. I was able to comply without any ill feelings or negative thoughts. I was able to maintain my peace by simply "letting it go."

Another good lesson in attachment came in 2000 when I was teaching Theosophy classes in Sarasota on Sunday mornings. For a time, my wife Beth joined in on the classes. One day she gave me some excellent feedback. She told me how I changed my demeanor and posture if someone challenged my beliefs or theosophical teachings. She said I would cross my arms over my chest and speak in a very defensive manner. I had not realized until then just how attached I was to my own opinions. I carefully examined my own thoughts and feelings and decided she was absolutely correct. It occurred to me that everyone feels the same way. We all want to feel secure in our beliefs, to feel we have a good handle on reality. We all want to feel as though our opinions are the correct ones. If we tell someone that they are dead wrong, they are likely to defend themselves by attacking us. No one wants the rug pulled out from underneath them. No one wants someone else's truth rammed down their throat. It occurred to me that my truths and opinions were constantly changing and evolving as I do. So how attached should I be to beliefs that are constantly changing? Since then I have become much more open-minded. The only belief I'm attached to now is, with God all things are possible!

Truth experienced is far superior to beliefs. I am open-minded to the truth of God's eternal presence here and now. All beliefs are rendered moot in the light of His presence. Beliefs about God are like a map to Paradise. The map is useful during the journey. However, once the destination has been reached, the map is no longer useful or necessary. To be open-minded is to be unattached to our beliefs. To overcome the illusion of duality, we must be open-minded to the Truth. We must be willing to let go of our illusions and embrace Truth, even if it is unsettling or downright scary. To traverse the Path that leads to true and lasting happiness, we must be willing to examine our beliefs about God, ourselves, the world around us, and our relationship with each.

Once we choose to seek Truth in our lives, we are on our way to experiencing a life filled with balance, harmony, peace and true and lasting happiness. Seek and you will find Him, ask for guidance and you will receive it, knock on God's door and He will open it, thirst for His right-use-ness, and you will be filled with wisdom.

CHAPTER 4

ILLUSION

How do we define illusion? According to one dictionary, illusion is "perception of something objectively existing in such a way as to cause misinterpretation of its actual nature." In other words, it's something having the appearance of realness, but without having any true substance. How about the word real? How do we define the word, *real*? The dictionary's definition is, "something genuine, not artificial, or illusory." It would be logical to say that real is the opposite of illusion. Something real has both image and substance, and something illusory has only the appearance of being real. A perfect example would be our reflection in a mirror. Image without substance.

How about a rainbow? Real or illusory? Well, it looks real enough. We can take a picture of it, right? Everyone sees the same thing. Usually we say that something out there, outside of us, that everyone can perceive is objectively real, correct? So is it? Our senses tell us it's real, right? However, science tells us it's an optical illusion caused by the sun's light rays passing through water droplets in the atmosphere. So, even though it appears real to our senses, a rainbow is an illusion because it has no true substance. Another feature of the rainbow is that it's not permanent, it's here one minute and disappears the next. An illusion is also something that is temporary or short-lived. A real thing has permanence.

How about magic? A magician's slight of hand uses real enough props.

Their maneuvers are impressive and realistic looking. Magicians are also called illusionists, right? What is the nature of a magician's illusions? Every trick involves a transformation, a change of some kind. We are either watching something disappear, or reappear. This is changed into that, or vice versa. We need to add to our definition of illusion, the concept of change. Things that are real are permanent, unchanging and have an image and substance.

Illusions in Our World

Imagine that you are standing on the shore of a large body of water, enjoying a beautiful sunset. Looking at the horizon stretching as far you can see, according to your observations using only your senses, does your world appear flat or round? Flat right? For the majority of the world's history, mankind believed the world to be flat. Why? Because we trust our senses. After all, if you played with water on the shore and noticed how it behaves, it reinforced the idea of the world being flat. If you had two children, and you gave one a plate and one a ball and asked each to fetch some water, only the child with a flat plate could bring back any water, right? It would make no sense to believe, based on your senses that the world is round. Water does not stay put on a round ball.

Now let's turn our attention toward the sun. Our senses observe the sun rising in the east and then setting in the west. Real or illusion? Our senses would logically suggest that the earth is stationary and the sun is revolving around us, right? This also was the popular belief before the advent of science. Science has proven that the sunrise and sunset are illusions. The truth is that the sun is stationary and earth is spinning and moving around it. Our senses of perception are actually quite limited and inaccurate. Our physical senses are not adequate to the task of perceiving truth. Actually they are quite adept at convincing us that illusions are real.

If science has proven the earth to be round, then how does the water of the oceans stay on it? Doesn't make sense. Science says its a mysterious force called gravity, and gravity holds the water and us firmly to the ground. Can our physical senses perceive gravity? We can usually perceive anything greater or less than 1G, as in acceleration, but not 1G. There is also a measurable force pushing down on us caused by miles and miles of moist air above us. Science calls this atmospheric pressure. Can our senses perceive atmospheric pressure? Not usually. However, older people with arthritis can tell when atmospheric pressure is changing, because of their aches and pains, but this is just the effect of change, not the pressure itself. Our bodies are pressurized internally to compensate for atmospheric pressure, so we don't feel it.

How about motion? Are your senses good at detecting motion? Let's test you. Sit back in your chair, close your eyes, take a deep breath and become as still as you can. Now, tell me, can you detect any motion within you? Perhaps. Some can detect their chests expanding with their breath. Some can feel their own heart beating. Some may detect movement within their bowels. A few are even sensitive enough to feel chi energy moving through their bodies. And although we may be able to detect our heart beating, we cannot perceive our blood pulsing throughout our bodies at considerable speed and pressure. We can sense heat or cold caused by blood circulation, but again this is only an effect of circulation, not the movement and pressure itself. Our senses may fool us into believing that there is stillness within us, when that is never the case.

Okay, now how about outside of you? Do you feel your body moving? Perfectly still? What if I were to tell you that in fact you are moving at a speed of approx. 1,000 miles per hour, right now? Impossible? While sitting here, none of us are currently moving relative to each other, but all of us are moving relative to the axis of the earth, at almost 1,000 miles per hour. But once again, we don't feel it. Are you starting to feel a little less confident in your ability to perceive the world around you accurately? Not only are we all moving relative to our earth's axis, we are also moving at incredible speed around our sun. And our entire solar system is moving at unimaginable speed relative to the center of our galaxy. And our galaxy is screaming away through space from all other galaxies. We are not in a static orbit around our sun. We are spiraling through regions of space we've never been in before. We are never still, even though our senses perceive otherwise.

Okay, forget motion. How about sight? Our eyes work well don't they? According to science, although our eyes relay about two million bits of information to our brain, our brain can only process less then 200,000 bits. So, even though there is a ton of information available to us, we can't perceive it all. Science has also proven that the brain sees only what it wants to see or expects to see. All new information is compared with old information—memories from the past. The past is like a filter through which our brains perceive the present moment. If you're extremely positive in nature then you will view the world through "rose-colored glasses." Everything is slightly distorted so as to be more acceptable. The more attached we are to the past, the muddier the filter is and the more distorted the present moment becomes. This is common among those suffering from anxiety and depression. The present moment is constantly being distorted into something fearful or negative. Instead of perceiving the present moment as it is, we see it slightly distorted, colored by the past.

We know that our human eyes are capable of perceiving everything in the visible light spectrum, right? However, the visible light spectrum is a tiny fraction of the total spectrum. There are colors below red, or infrared, and colors above violet or ultraviolet. If the entire spectrum of light could be symbolized by a keyboard, the visible light spectrum would represent one octave or about seven inches. The entire keyboard, however, would stretch from New York to San Francisco. Incredible! So now what do you think of our physical senses? No wonder God can forgive us so easily—we are practically blind, stumbling around in the dark. Our five physical senses are lame!

Just think about it. Our physical eyes perceive only a tiny fraction of the realities existing within the entire light spectrum. We are completely oblivious to other spectrums, frequencies, dimensions and universes. Add to that, our physical brain can only perceive a tiny fraction of what's happening in our own spectrum, in the world right in front of us. And of that tiny fraction that we do see, we don't see clearly! We are easily lied to and easily fooled by misdirection and slight of hand. We misinterpret what's happening right in front of us, and we suffer endlessly from misunderstandings.

What is the source of all this confusion? The source is our limited senses. We never seem to get the whole picture. What does the brain do with the missing pieces? It fills them in with guess work and fantasy. Once we fall prey to the workings of our minds and believe in our illusions, we then become delusional. Our own delusions are the source of our suffering. Most suffering is self inflicted. We suffer from our endless wants and desires our attachments and obsessions but most of all, our suffering stems from a misunderstanding of reality or truth. Everyone has their own belief system, their own personal paradigm, their own unique way perceiving the world around them. Beliefs are often shared, but rarely are they identical. So, if everyone believes differently, how do we know what is truth? I believe that what's true for God is the one Truth. But since we can never know the entire mind of God or His ultimate Truth, the next best thing we can do is to compare our personal truths with Universal Truth. Universal Truths are discussed at length later in the chapter on Rules.

There is another issue I would like to discuss now. I believe this illusion, this misunderstanding, causes the greatest amount of suffering to mankind. This grand illusion is Death.

The Illusion of Death

It was at this point that I took pause in writing this book. I really wasn't sure how I should approach this tender subject, so I went within myself and asked the Omnipresent Spirit of God for some help. Some wisdom, guidance, a miracle, anything. The next day at work, I had a new client on my schedule, Ms. Jean K. While taking her medical history, we had the following conversation.

"My whole body hurts. My doctor has diagnosed me with fibromyalgia. Do you know what that is?"

"Yes, it is a systemic pain disorder. It's really a syndrome, which means its a common problem. However we don't quite understand what the root cause is or how to treat it effectively, so fibromyalgia is a known name for an unknown problem."

"I also suffer from a rare blood disease. I'm prone to both clotting and bleeding issues at the same time. The doctors say that should be impossible, however, here I am. They say I should have died years ago. I'm well past my expiration date. As a matter of fact, I did die!"

"Really!? Can you tell me more about that?"

"Well, it happened back in 1976, shortly after having given birth to my second son. The nurse was checking in on me every hour, but between visits all the blood drained out of my body, and into the hospital bed. I remember clearly, feeling my chronic intense pain leaving me in an instant. I felt wonderful, better than I ever had in my entire life. I remember being suspended in the room, hovering over my corpse lying there in a huge pool of blood. Strangely enough, I wasn't the least bit concerned about this. I was experiencing an ever increasing feeling of peace—I was okay—everything was okay. Next I saw the nurse scramble to my side and I heard her screaming for the doctor. I hear, "No pulse! I'm getting no pulse!!" The next thing I saw is what I remember most vividly—I see it clearly even now. It was a look of abject horror on the face of my doctor. His face was drained of blood and his mouth hung agape. I really thought he was going to keel over and die right there. You have to understand that the doctor was also a personal friend. We had just played bridge together a few nights earlier. So I'm looking at him, thinking to myself, *Steve, relax, it's okay. I'm fine. As a matter of fact, I'm great!* I then felt overwhelmed with intense peace, love and joy. I saw a brilliant light up above, and I started floating towards it. Then, I heard as clear as day, a booming voice. In a somewhat stern manner say, **"Not Yet!"** A moment later, I was back in my body, my doctor had succeeded in reviving me by pumping artificial blood into me. You see, all my veins had collapsed. It took years of transfusions to get me full of real blood again. Later when I recounted my experience to my doctor friend, he just shook his head and said "Nope, sorry. I'm a doctor and a scientist I just cant bring myself to believe you." I got the same kind of response from my husband as well."

"Wow! That's quite a story Jean. But you know what? I believe you 100%. Why? Because I also had an experience of death. Thirteen years ago, in the early morning hours of Christmas Eve, I died in my hot tub. I remember clearly having a conversation with Jesus. During the conversation at one point, I remember offering to do the Lord's work here on earth. I felt something touch the top of my head. I then experienced what I can only describe as a high speed download. I saw my entire life flash before my eyes in mere moments. Then again, another set of a rapidly flashing images before my closed eyes. This time, however, these were images of a life yet to live. A moment later I woke up in my hot tub completely unaware of my experience with God, climbed out of the spa and went to bed. It took a few weeks before I could consciously remember the experience. I lived in a constant state of spiritual bliss for the next forty days. I felt entirely reborn. I've spent the last thirteen years trying to understand and integrate my spiritual experiences."

"You know what? Ever since that experience some thirty-five years ago, I have had absolutely no fear of death."

"Yes! Me too! Isn't it wonderful!?"

"It's very comforting to know that there really is no death. No loss of awareness, knowledge or memories. We remain ourselves and continue on. On to a new life and new experiences."

"I agree completely. In fact, after the fear of death disappears, so do many other fears. At this point, I experience very little fear in my life."

"Yes," says Jean, "that intense peace I felt could be described as the absence of any fear whatsoever. It's beautiful beyond words. I think often about that amazing feeling, I want to experience it some more. I'll even go so far as to say the unthinkable, I look forward to my death! I embrace it. However, the words "Not yet," imply that my life has purpose and meaning. It makes living with constant physical pain that much more bearable. I know that my body and my pain are temporary and that my life is eternal. I had one more daughter a few years later, so I figured that she was my purpose. I keep expecting to die, but here I am! Guess I have yet more work to do. So I wait patiently."

"That's awesome, Jean! I'm so glad we met. Like you, I've had much difficulty convincing people too. I've yet to meet anyone who shares my understanding of life after death. It's such a shame that so many live in painful ignorance. The knowledge of the illusion of death is indeed the truth that shall set you free."

"I couldn't agree more!"

Although Jean and I had only just met, the look we shared told me we had made a deep connection. It told me we that we would always be friends. The expression on her face and the gleam in her eyes expressed a silent "Namaste," an ancient Indian greeting, translated as, "The omnipresent spirit of God that resides within me, recognizes the omnipresent spirit of God residing in you." We share an extremely rare gift. We both experienced death, and lived to tell about it. We hold the key to the mother of all mysteries. We know the Truth. We know that we are not our bodies. We know that it is only our body that dies. We are Sons and Daughters of a living God. We live eternally. We know that death is just a shift in awareness not unlike waking up or falling asleep. We wake up in Unity consciousness, one with God, and yet we still have our individuality. And in that sphere of consciousness, there exists only Peace, only Love, only Joy, only oneness and understanding. Oneness with your Father, one with the entire universe. Unity with God is like the word ineffable, too holy to be described with words.

Okay, so now the Truth is out there. How long will you deny it? It took a long time for people to come around to the idea of the world being round, rather than flat. After all, their own physical senses perceive it as such. It also took a long time for people to accept the Truth that the sun is stationary and it is we who are traveling around it. Why? Once again, our senses confuse us. Our senses are inadequate to the task of perceiving reality accurately.

So, what do our senses tell us about death? They perceive nothing. We're left to think it is total annihilation—the end. Remember earlier we talked about the light spectrum, and how our eyes can perceive only a tiny portion of that spectrum? The Lord is Life and Light. The entire spectrum is teaming with life. We go on from here. We take our experiences, our lessons learned, our memories, and our love connections. Death is simply awakening into a different reality. And life continues ....

What Is Real?

Okay, we've looked at some samples of illusions. Reflections in a mirror, magician's slight of hand, rainbows and sunsets. So what is real? Search your mind, and see if you can come up with an example of something that has image and substance, doesn't end, and doesn't change. Come up with anything yet? This is difficult isn't it? Doesn't change? Everything in this world is in a constant state of change, isn't it?

How about our beliefs? Every choice we make, every action we undertake is based on our beliefs, right? They feel very real, but they do, however, change.

How about our feelings? They are the most real thing to us, aren't they? Pain especially feels VERY real. But once again, our feelings and emotions are in a constant state of flux and change.

How about our experiences? All experience is in the past. The past only has existence within our minds. We cannot relive the past, we can only experience a memory or reproduction of the past, but it is still experienced in the present moment. The past is an illusion.

How about memories? If we forget something that happened in the past, then it no longer exists for us, right? However our soul keeps a permanent record of everything we experience here on earth, so really, our memories are real and eternal. Memories can be a constant source of pain, can't they? Consider this, the more real we consider our experiences, the greater the feeling and emotion attached to it, right? The greater the pain, the guilt and the heartache. My point is this. If we can accept that our experiences are not as real as we think they are, then we will experience less pain associated with them. When we constantly remind ourselves that things, events, and feelings are temporary and illusory, then we can attain a greater degree of peace in our lives. If we say to ourselves, this too shall pass, then the pain we experience is lessened somewhat. This is the benefit to understanding the illusory nature of existence—greater peace.

How about Love? Now we're getting somewhere. Love is

very real. Real love is eternal and unchanging. It transcends time and space. Our memories and love connections are the only things we get to take with us when we leave this earth. What's the point in pursuing money, fame and influence. We can't take them with us. They are unimportant in the big picture. Our lives should instead be spent making beautiful memories, and developing real love for others and God.

How about the world of objects outside of us? It looks and feels very real and permanent doesn't it? However, even the Egyptian pyramids, the most permanent of all physical structures are decaying, slowly eroding over time. What lasts forever? The earth itself perhaps? Science says our sun will die some day and so will this planet and all life thereon. So what is real?

In my opinion, that which best fits our definition of the word "real", of having image and substance, unchanging and eternal, is God Himself. God is eternal, unchanging and perfect. His image is Light, his substance is Life.

What about us? Well, our bodies certainly change constantly and then die. Our bodies are illusory, temporary. But we are real. We are Sons and Daughters of God. We are light, we are eternal consciousness, we are perfect and unchanging just as our Heavenly Father is perfect and unchanging. Our experiences don't change who we are in essence, they only change how we perceive ourselves. Our earthly experiences lead us eventually to the Truth. We are not human beings having spiritual experiences, we are rather spiritual beings having a human experience.

Actually, there is something on this planet, that meets the criteria for being real. This is deoxyribonucleic acid or DNA. It's been on this planet for millions of years, as long as there has been life. It has an image, the double-helix spiral.

It's substance is huge amounts of information. It replicates itself eternally, and has remained essentially unchanged over millennia.

Are dreams real? We all know that dreams are mere fantasy, just workings of the subconscious mind, right? Have you ever had a nightmare? Have you ever had a dream that frightened you out of your wits? Did you wake up in a panic, heart racing, drenched with sweat? Did your fear linger even though you were safe in your bed? Did you ever stop to think about how real dreams are when you're in one, especially a scary dream? Within your dream, you are aware and awake, perceiving your environment, and cognizing what you see, right? For all intents and purposes this experience is real. After all, we have a body in the dream and we are using all our senses. And our physical body is reacting according to the nature of the dream. If its scary, our body responds to our dreams accordingly. Our respiratory and heart rate increases and we perspire. If it is a sensual or sexual dream, we become aroused. And let's face it, we don't realize we're in a dream until we wake up! We have to first shift our angle of perception, before we can perceive the illusion. Waking up from a dream, and exiting your physical vehicle at the time of passing, are practically the same experience. A shift in awareness. From sleeping to waking, from duality to Unity. Feels the same. Our sense of Self is eternal. Even within your dreams you are always you. Our experience of individuality is unending, eternal. Throughout this life and in the hereafter.

Do you like magic? Most do, some don't. For some, magic disturbs them greatly. They don't like change, they don't like having their core beliefs about reality challenged. They need things to be steady and predictable. Rattle their cage too much and they are likely to react violently. Why are they like this? The root cause is attachment. We can become overly attached to our beliefs. When our core beliefs are challenged, we feel as if our very lives are at risk. We defend our old beliefs even when new and better information comes along. We're too slow to change our minds. The more open-minded we are, the easier it is to shift to alternate perspectives, alternative view points. Open-minded people love magic, they love new and interesting possibilities and experiences. But, whether were open-minded or not, magicians and illusionists have little trouble fooling our senses. Think about it, we easily fall prey to a little misdirection and slight of hand. Our friends can look us in the eye and tell us a bold-face lie and we believe it. Our senses are lame! They are constantly fooling us into thinking that illusions are real. Reflections and shadows, rainbows, sunrise and sunset, and dreams. We cannot trust only our physical senses for interpreting reality. If we do, we are like the blind leading the blind, likely to fall into a pit.

Okay, okay, you say, our senses are extremely limited. What choice do we have? They are all we have to work with, right? What can we do about it? How do we navigate through life without falling into a pit of delusions?

Surrender!

CHAPTER 5

SURRENDER

One dictionary defines *surrender* as, "To give oneself over to another's influence." Usually when we think of the word, surrender, we think of perhaps a war, where the losing army surrenders. This brings with it associated thoughts of failure, submission, humiliation and perhaps even slavery. This is not the kind of surrender to which I am referring. The definition, "To give oneself over to another's influence" still applies, however, the difference is that we are surrendering unto God's influence.

Why would we want to surrender to God's influence? When we finally realize just how limited our physical senses are, we also realize that we need better ways to navigate through life, avoiding unnecessary strife.

In the past we have compensated for our shortcomings by building tools to make labor easier. Scientists used their creative imaginations to develop technology. Who today doesn't enjoy a life enriched with technology? We are all addicted to our wireless devices. Don't we watch the weather channel so we're prepared for inclement weather? Don't we love to use our GPS systems in our cars, so we don't get lost or stuck in traffic? Don't we just love to heat up our food in a few minutes or less in our microwaves? Don't we just love to keep up with all our friends on Facebook and Twitter? What did we do before Google? Open a book? Go to the library? The internet makes available anything you want to know, any place you wish to see, anybody you wish to speak with. The World Wide Web is revolutionizing this planet. We now have a global communications network and a global marketplace. We can now communicate with and purchase from any person or business on the planet in real time.

Technology is wonderful. It acts as an extension of our physical senses, allowing us to perceive more of the world around us. It also allows us to see just how limited our five physical senses are in perceiving this reality. But do we realize just how much we "give ourselves over to the influence of" technology? When we surrender ourselves over to technology, we just might do so at the expense of our own personal power. We can no longer do for ourselves. We become slaves to it. Let me give you an example. The other day, I was sitting in a fast food drive-through, in front of the speaker box. I waited patiently for someone to ask for my order. After a long time, I finally cleared my throat a few times then said "Hello"? A young man's voice came over the speaker.

"I'm sorry sir, my computer is down, so I can't take your order."

I said, "Excuse me? Can't you just write down what I want and figure out the price?"

"Nope! Sorry, sir."

I drove away dumbfounded. He had no personal power with which to take a simple meal order. Without his technology he was powerless, unable to think or do anything, like a deer in the headlights. Similarly, it seems as though people working the register in retail shops have forgotten how to count back change. They have to rely on calculators. With the advent of texting, young people are also losing their verbal and handwriting skills. When we surrender to technology, it comes at tremendous cost, our own personal power. We become weaker, not stronger, even though it may appear the other way around. When we surrender to God and His influence, the cost is our illusions. We are empowered, not enslaved. After we surrender to Him, we have far more power and potential than we ever would have with technology alone.

When we surrender to God, He showers us with His divine Love, Wisdom, Guidance and Protection. And, His guidance and protection is endless, eternal, reliable in the extreme. Technology on the other hand, not so much. It is a very real possibility that someday soon, a huge solar flare will wipe out all orbiting satellites and decimate world power grids. Imagine being instantly transported back to the 19th century, in a manner of speaking. No electricity, no computers, nada. It's frightening to think about and yet it could very well happen. We need to maintain our ability to function in this world with or without technology.

How Do We Surrender?

How do we surrender? Carrie Underwood has a hit song entitled, *Jesus take the wheel*. In the song, a woman is driving in her car with her baby sleeping in the back seat. Suddenly, she hits a patch of ice and her car starts to spin out of control. During the spin, she realizes that she is no longer in control and she prays to Jesus to "take the wheel."

This is an act of surrender. What makes it a true act of surrender is her sincerity. She knew in that instant, that she was absolutely powerless, so she completely surrendered her fate to the all powerful and merciful Lord. She prayed that He would intervene on her behalf with a miracle. In the song, she does indeed stop without incident, her baby still sleeping in the back seat.

Sincerity is the key. The Omnipresent indwelling Lord of the universe, knows you better than you know yourself. He hears your thoughts, He knows your dreams and goals, and He knows your fears and weaknesses. He loves us so much He has given us the ultimate gift, the gift of free will. This means He will not interfere in our lives unless we ask Him to do so. To surrender our free will and receive His help and guidance, we must sincerely want a relationship with Him. We must have a burning desire for His Wisdom, Guidance, Love and Protection. We have to honestly believe that He is far more capable of directing our lives than are we. Only He knows the Truth. We are stumbling around in the dark, confused by a world of illusions. He is a far better navigator than we are.

God is like a good tour guide—He takes us where we want to go and educates us along the way. His Path is the right path. His Path leads to true and lasting happiness, here and now. God is like the GPS in our vehicles, guiding us back to the right Path after we have lost our way.

Most of us do just what the woman in Carrie's song probably did. We surrender to God in the midst of crisis, however, once the crisis has passed, we once again desire to take back the wheel, be in control again and continue on being our own guide through life. Because of free will, the Lord has no choice but to relinquish control back to us. To practice true surrender, it must become a habit, a state of mind, something we practice on a daily basis. Every day we have to say to God, "Not mine, but Thy will be done." For God to become our true guide in life, we must be constantly surrendering unto Him. We have to remind ourselves repeatedly, that He is all knowing. He knows what's best for us and as a loving Father, He wants what's best for us. We have to trust in His Goodness and believe that with His guidance, we will walk the path in life with the least amount of pain and suffering. Perfect surrender is complete surrender.

Our Heavenly Father wants a very personal relationship with each of us. He is not content with anything less than our full attention. He doesn't want us to think of Him only in times of crisis or once a week on Sundays. He wants us to talk to Him incessantly, and rely on Him completely.

Persistence is another important key to success. Remember, God is our Father. He is our parent. Any parent can ignore a crying child for a time, however, a persistent cry always gets a parent's attention. To get God's attention, we have to make a lot of noise. If we persistently and sincerely surrender our control, surrender our hopes and dreams, surrender our fears and doubts, then we are sure to experience His presence. If we persistently and sincerely ask Him to, He will reveal Himself to us. He will fill our hearts with His Love and Happiness, our minds with His Wisdom and Peace, and our bodies with His Light. He will help us to perceive Truth in a world of illusions. Pain and suffering will diminish, peace, love and joy will reign supreme. We will walk through the valley of the shadow of death and yet fear no evil, for the Lord is with us, always and forever.

No man is capable of fully knowing God, Yet all men are capable of experiencing His presence. Seek within, and we will find Him, Ask for His guidance, and we will receive it, Knock and the door will be opened to us, Thirst for His right-use-ness, and we will be filled with His Wisdom.

Once we succeed in this endeavor, our lives will never be the same. How will we know that we have been successful? We experience an emotion that is beyond our wildest imaginations. That emotion is real Happiness. There are no words in existence capable of expressing this emotion. Words like joy, bliss and ecstasy, don't even come close. Once we experience God's Love and its associated Happiness, there will be no doubt that we have successfully achieved our aim.

CHAPTER 6

HAPPINESS

The founding fathers of this great nation, when drafting the Declaration of Independence wrote, "All men are created equal, endowed by their Creator with certain unalienable rights, such as life, liberty and the pursuit of happiness." The authors of the Gettysburg address wrote "Four score and seven years ago, our fathers brought forth on this continent a new nation, conceived in Liberty and dedicated to the proposition that all men are created equal."

They believed then, as I do today, that all men and woman are indeed created equal. We are all God's children, each one of us, created in His image and likeness. We are immortal souls, vessels of His eternal consciousness. We are perfect as our Heavenly Father is perfect. We are Life eternal as He is Life eternal. His essence is our essence.

I believe that no soul is more special or better than any other soul. We are all equally perfect. And yet, each one of us is entirely unique. No two souls have shared the exact same life experiences, therefore, we are unique and yet the same. A rose is a rose, regardless of its color. Each soul is perfect, and yet colored by its experiences. In our society, instead of conforming or trying to be like others, we should instead embrace our uniqueness.

There is obviously abundant life on this planet with a global population approaching seven billion. Over the last few decades, we have witnessed a tremendous surge of freedoms, starting with the fall of communism and the Berlin wall, and most recently with the ousting of several Mideastern dictators. So, plenty of life and liberty, but where are all the happy people? Seems as if we are all still in the "pursuit of happiness," doesn't it?

Is real happiness attainable? Does it really exist? Or is it just the proverbial carrot on a stick? In my mind, I see a cartoon strip. In the first frame is a rat running—in the "rat race," of course—and strapped to its back is a pole and a string, and dangling in his face is a carrot. Down the length of the carrot it reads, "Happiness." In the second frame, the rat becomes disillusioned and stops to sit by the side of the road to rest in a bed of roses. He notices, however, that while in a seated position, the carrot is right in his face within reach. In the third frame, we see the rat lounging peacefully among the roses with a broad smile on his face. There is a chunk of the carrot missing and it now reads ""Happi."

Can you relate to this? Are you genuinely happy or are you always in the pursuit of happiness? Is it always just seemingly out of reach? Perhaps you are just putting it off for now, while you focus on other things? Is happiness something you hope to attain in the future? Are you expecting to find happiness once you find that perfect mate? Perhaps you are waiting for that job promotion or the day you open your own business? Maybe you don't expect to find happiness until you own your own home or have your own children. Or perhaps you are waiting for financial success and security? Maybe you believe that happiness is to be experienced in retirement?

WHAT IS THE SOURCE OF HAPPINESS?

I used to think that pleasure and happiness were more or less synonymous. I used to think that pleasure in abundance led to happiness. It was for this reason that I overindulged in sensual pleasures. I had no idea that my unhappiness and depression were a direct result of my overindulgences.

I did not know the Truth that the path that leads to pleasure is not the path to happiness. Comparing pleasure to happiness is like comparing a light bulb to the sun. Their only similarity is that they are both a source of light. The difference in intensity and quality of light, however, are beyond compare.

Before a comparison can be made, one must first experience Divine Joy or true and lasting Happiness. The only way to experience true and lasting Happiness is to come to know the Truth for yourself that God is here now. How do we do this? Simply make a persistent, sincere plea to the indwelling Lord that He make Himself known to your heart and mind, so that you can both hear His divine Word, and feel His divine Peace, Love and Joy in your heart and body. Think about this. Then ask yourself the following questions:

- How long does happiness last after we purchase the things we desire?

- Is it possible to desire something that you already possess?

- How long does happiness last from a conquest in competition?

- How long does a gold medal bring happiness?

- Are you still serene and relaxed from your previous vacation? How long did that last?

- Is that excellent dinner from last night still bringing you pleasure or happiness?

- Is sex entirely satiating or are you always left wanting more?

No sensual indulgence can bring lasting happiness. The pleasure or happiness experienced as a result of sensual indulgence is fleeting! Only the happiness that results from Love is lasting. Only after we have experienced the divine intensity of pure satisfaction can we then let go of our need for sensual pleasures. Our egos want us to be addicted to comfort, luxury and excess in food, clothes, drugs, money and sex. Our true Selves need only bask in light of God's Love and Grace to easily put aside all selfishness.

In the light of God's Light, we feel whole and complete, no lack of any kind. It's as if there is nothing more to do and nothing left undone. We feel we are in the right place at the right time, doing exactly what we are supposed to be doing. There is no feeling of inadequacy or unworthiness, fear or doubt. We experience genuine desirelessness. We feel no need to compete, no need to consume, no need to collect and no need to control. When we connect with the indwelling Lord, we never feel alone or lonely again. He becomes our constant companion, making us feel connected, accepted, fulfilled and loved unconditionally. No prescription drug can do that. No psychotropic drug can do that. No amount of money can buy that. No amount over overindulgence can compare with it. Nothing on earth can bring lasting happiness like your Father's Love and amazing Grace!

God is Love. Love is happiness. To know God is to know happiness. God is here now. God is within us. Think about it, we have within us, right now, an inexhaustible supply of love. This Love is free to us, and yet it is the currency with which we pay our Karmic debt to the universe. It is not necessary to acquire anything. We just love abundantly and abundant Love comes to us. We receive in equal measure to what we give. Give abundantly! And you will surely receive true and lasting happiness.

Based on the current divorce rate of 50%, it sounds reasonable to suggest that most people feel it is the primary responsibility of their spouse to make them happy. When they fall short of accomplishing this, we toss them aside in favor of someone else who might do a better job.

Many college students change their major several times because they don't feel their current endeavor will bring happiness. We jump from job to job, career to career, hoping to find just the right one that will bring us happiness. We make endless trips to the mall, hoping that if we surround ourselves with luxury and comfort, adorn ourselves with pretty things, we will know happiness. Some work from dawn till dusk trying to attain that magic bank balance, the one that brings them peace, security and happiness.

I think most people are convinced that more money will make them happy. However if you closely observe rich people, you will quickly come to the conclusion that rich people are no happier than anyone else. Money can bring comfort, security and pleasure, but not happiness. I learned this lesson early on because of my high school buddy, Steve. He had the most personality, natural charm and charisma of anyone I've ever known. Steve was very driven to be successful and happy. It didn't take him long to earn his first million. He admitted to me that once he reached his goal of one million dollars in assets, he fell short of achieving happiness. He decided that it must take two million dollars to make someone truly happy, so he set out to make more money. I was jealous of his money and success, which is why I was so surprised by his comments when I admitted as much while we were having chicken wings and beer at the local, original Hooters restaurant. Steve admitted that it was he who was envious of *my* life! I couldn't believe my ears. He told me that even though he had tons of cash and a luxury sports car and a huge home, every day he came home from work to an empty house. He had come to realize that all the luxurious possessions and sensual indulgences in the world could never bring us real and lasting happiness. From his perspective, I appeared much happier, because I had so much love in my life. I married my high school sweetheart, had three beautiful sons and worked in a family business. Even though we struggled financially, Steve envied my lifestyle. I believe it was a great lesson for both of us. Because of him, I didn't have to waste my life learning that valuable lesson. Thank you, Steve!

Many people believe that they can acquire happiness through food. If this were the case, then obese people would be the happiest among us, and I'm sure you don't think that is the case. Food can bring us a measure of contentment, but not happiness.

Some believe happiness can be found in a pill or intoxicating drink. If this were the case than drunks and drug addicts would be the happiest among us. Are they? Certainly not! I'm sure we could agree that they suffer greatly. Drugs can bring only temporary pleasure, followed by lingering pain and suffering. Drugs can never bring us lasting happiness, no matter how much we overindulge.

Many believe happiness can be attained through sex. On

the surface it may appear that sex addicts are the happiest among us, however, this is an illusion. Sex addicts suffer as much as drug addicts, food addicts and those obsessed with money.

So if we can't find true and lasting happiness through money, food, drugs or sex, then what is the cause of happiness? I'll give you a hint. How do you spot someone in love? They are exceedingly happy, right? Truth is, the cause of happiness is love. Love is the cause, happiness is the effect. Cause and effect. Any act of love and kindness will bring a measure of joy or happiness. Simple enough isn't it? Selfish indulgence of the senses, brings only pleasure and pain, selfless acts of love and kindness bring real and lasting happiness. In the Bible, God promises to reward any act of love and kindness done in secret. The reward is happiness! Don't take my word for it, experiment with it yourself. Make the choice each and every day to do a kindness to a stranger and tell no one. You will certainly experience an increase in joy and happiness in your life.

How Do We Attain Happiness?

Want more happiness in your life? Be kind to everyone you meet! Even the smallest gestures of love and kindness can bring you some joy. When you come face to face with a stranger, greet them with a smile. A genuine smile is an act of love and kindness. If it's appropriate, give them a compliment. Doesn't it feel good when someone gives you a compliment? That good feeling is joy. Spread it around. When you leave their presence, send them off with a blessing. For example, suggest they have a wonderful day, or wish them good luck, or say God bless you! And then leave them with another genuine smile. If you do this to everyone you meet, you will gain a measure of happiness in your life.

Want more happiness in your life? Then become a volunteer! Help those less fortunate than yourself, and you will know happiness. The happiest people you are ever going to meet are those engaged in selfless service to their fellow man. Selfish actions only bring temporary pleasure followed by pain and suffering, never happiness. We cannot make ourselves happy by fulfilling our selfish desires. I'm not suggesting that one or two good deeds will bring endless happiness. To attain true and lasting happiness, we need to give more than we take on a daily basis. With every single encounter we have with another person, we are given the opportunity to sow future seeds of either suffering or happiness. The choice is always ours. Free will, remember? And with every exchange, we are also given the opportunity to grow and advance spiritually. We are all in this together, as one. We cannot learn or grow, or achieve happiness without each other. This world provides endless opportunities for expressing compassion, mercy and love. And that is exactly what is required of us to experience any happiness. If we are living alone, and not interacting with our fellow man, we are cutting ourselves off from our own happiness.

Want more happiness in your life? If you are living alone, miserable and depressed, adopt a pet! Go down to your local shelter and rescue some poor animal that is homeless and on death row. Bring it home and bathe it, feed it, walk it and love it! Do this, and your pet will bring you some happiness. God is like a good dog, He desires to serve you well, is fiercely loyal and offers unconditional love even if you are selfish, obnoxious or ugly. Dogs can be very adept at teaching us how to love unconditionally. God is also like a good cat, perfectly content to wait for you to come to Him. When you do come before Him, surrender your free will in favor of His wisdom, guidance and protection, then you are in line to experience the ultimate happiness.

Want more happiness in your life? Surrender your life to God! There is no greater happiness than that experienced as a direct result of God's love for us. When we say to God daily, "Thy will be done," this makes Him very happy, and He then gives us more of His love. When God expresses His Love for us, we experience a level of happiness that is beyond words. Joy, bliss and ecstasy don't even come close to describing this indescribable emotion. This Happiness is unending and eternal. Even in the midst of drama and crisis, His Happiness remains. His Love and it's associated Happiness is real, true and lasting. Surrender to the omnipresent Lord residing within you. His Love and Happiness is available to you right here, right now. Don't wait for the future, for the future is an illusion. In reality, we only ever have the present moment, here and now. **GOD IS HERE NOW!**

Your Heavenly Father is waiting for you. If your desire is strong enough and your heart is sincere enough, if you are humble and persistent enough, He will reveal Himself to you, and you will know the ultimate Happiness!

CAN WE MAKE OURSELVES HAPPY?

YES! We can make ourselves happy. Actually, this is a great place to start, if you have little to no happiness in your life right now. How? First, we have to abandon our guilt. Guilt is not a useful emotion. As a matter of fact, it is a barrier to happiness. Guilt is a manmade construct, designed to gain control over others. Its premise is that our selfish acts will anger or offend God. This is an illusion, an impossibility. God is pure and perfect Love. He gives only unconditional Love and Forgiveness. To believe that God could be angry, vengeful, punishing and wrathful is to believe in a God created in our image and likeness. It's "As above, so below," not the other way around. Unity exists within duality, not the other way around. And one exists within two, not the other way around.

We are like God, in essence, He is not like us, subject to the illusions of Duality. If you knew for a fact that God is going to Love you and forgive you, regardless of your transgressions, would you still hold on to your guilt? He doesn't want us to be unhappy and guilt ridden, He wants us to be happy and to love one another. This is why we are here. We have to learn how to give abundantly, love unconditionally and forgive everyone and everything, just as He does.

Forgiveness *is* an act of love and kindness. This act of love can be directed towards yourself or others. Either way, it will bring a measure of joy into our lives. Guilt is like a big sack of bricks that we drag around with us, holding us back. We need to just set it down and walk away. It lowers our vibration and saps our energy. It even has the potential to make us ill. It is a useless, negative, destructive emotion. Guilt does not serve us well in any way. We need to change our thinking. This is the first step towards Happiness.

When we are filled with guilt, we tend to act out against ourselves. We deprive ourselves of the good things in life as self-punishment. We can become negative, depressed or even self-destructive. This is NOT what God wants for us. He wants us to forgive ourselves and find happiness. Self-abuse only leads to unhappiness. Self-love can lead to happiness. We have to realize however that self-love is NOT the same as self-indulgence. Self-love is accepting yourself as you are, without condemnation or judgments. It's also being open to having fun, enjoying the good things in life and finding friendship and love. Self-love is recognizing yourself as a perfect child of God. And your Heavenly Father loves you more than you could possibly imagine.

**Love yourself and God,
and you will surely know Happiness.**

Want more happiness in your life? Create a gratitude journal! Too often we tend to focus too much on what we don't have, rather than what we do have. We are very desirous beings. We are constantly looking for that next thing to possess, that special thing that will make us happy. There is a very simple exercise that will create more happiness for us. We need to sit down and make a list, an inventory of everything that we currently have in our lives. It should be a list of things we like, appreciate and want to keep. Don't leave anything out. Include family and friends, your life partner, your job, possessions, everything. Then every single day, read the list. As you go through the list, give thanks to God for bringing this into your life. If we give thanks daily for all the blessings in our lives, we will surely know more happiness. Developing the attitude of gratitude is an excellent way to create happiness. Why? Because expressing gratitude is an act of love and kindness. When it is directed towards God, He returns our love with His Love. And His Love is the greatest source of real and lasting Happiness. However, gratitude directed towards other people is also very effective. Don't you experience a measure of joy when someone expresses gratitude towards you? God is like any good parent, He enjoys watching His children display humility, obedience and gratitude.

Want more happiness in your life? Practice lovemaking! I said earlier that happiness cannot be attained through sex. This is true most of the time, however, there is an exception. So what is the difference between sex and lovemaking? On the surface, they would appear to be the very same act. The difference is in the intention or the energy behind the act. If the intention is to fulfill a lustful desire, then the act is selfish. The energy behind the fulfillment of natural physical urges is a much lower vibration that that of expressing real love. If we are taking pleasure from someone else, we are being selfish and we will not experience happiness. If our intention is to express real love, then we are giving, not taking. While engaged in true lovemaking, energy is flowing out from us. When we are taking pleasure in sex, energy is flowing towards us. Do you see the difference? Sex is selfish, lovemaking is selfless. Real lovemaking is an act of love and kindness that will create happiness. In true lovemaking, no one is taking anything. Rather than taking, we are allowing ourselves to receive. This may appear to be a distinction without a difference, but really it is quite profound. Allowing yourself to receive is being open and energetically neutral or passive. Energy is still flowing towards us, however, we are not actively taking anything. We can't take a gift—we can only receive it. In lovemaking, each partner takes turn focusing on giving pleasure only, while their partner passively receives that pleasure. To make love is to selflessly give pleasure to your partner with an open heart. Lovemaking is not just the sex act. Lovemaking should include the giving of gifts, feeding each other, bathing each other, giving each other compliments. All happily married couples know this to be true. If you want more happiness in your marriage, make love as often as possible.

Want more happiness in your life? Stop watching the news! Think about this. It was not until recent decades, with the advent of global communications, that people were subject to daily barrages of negative news from around the globe. Is it any wonder that so many millions of people are suffering from anxiety and depression? For the first six thousand years of our history, people only had to deal with the issues within their own families and communities. Only the ruler of the country was forced to deal with every tragedy happening within his kingdom. Nowadays, we get to watch every horrible thing happening in the entire world. This is NOT our responsibility! Not only that, but it is detrimental to our emotional health and well-being. Two thousand years ago, there was no TV or global communications and Jesus said to those around Him (Matthew 10:19), "Therefore, do not worry about tomorrow, for tomorrow will worry about itself. *Each day has enough trouble of its own.*" Our own lives are filled with enough drama and pain. We were never meant to take on the troubles of the whole world. Stop watching the news and you will have less anxiety and depression.

We can take this one step further. To have more happiness in our lives, we should try to watch only positive, uplifting, inspiring shows on television. Why? Because we can attain some happiness just by witnessing acts of love and kindness! Yes, this is true. Have you ever been to a wedding? Those witnessing the event shed tears of joy, do they not? God is like a wedding, the epitome of Love and Happiness. Two hearts and minds joined as one in the sight of God, family and friends. Lots of food and drink, music and dance. God is like a good song, inspiring us to sing and dance, and celebrate the joy of life. It's a very beautiful experience. Have you ever watched the TV show, *Extreme Makeover: Home*

Edition? This show should convince you of the Truth that just witnessing an act of love and kindness can create real joy. Good and deserving people, who are down and out and desperately in need, are given an entirely new home, free of charge, fully equipped with every modern convenience. Hundreds of people volunteer their time and money in this venture. At the end of the show, when they have the big reveal, we are witness to extreme, genuine happiness and gratitude. One's heart cannot help but be touched by this.

Here is my suggestion. If you are suffering from anxiety and depression, take a break from watching the news or reading the newspaper for two weeks. And during that time, allow yourself to watch only romantic comedies and shows like *Extreme Home Makeover*. Read uplifting and inspiring books. Bombard your consciousness with only good and happy things, and you will have more happiness in your life. I promise!

Want more happiness in your life? Embrace balance! A balanced day for instance would include eight hours of work, eight hours of sleep and eight hours of fun or relaxation. This is obviously an ideal, however, to have a balanced life, we should strive to attain this to the best of our ability. If we are working twelve or more hours a day, having little fun and even less sleep, then happiness will certainly elude us. Remember, money can bring pleasure, security and comforts, but *never* happiness. If we are working very little, getting loads of sleep and spending the majority of our time engaged in the pursuit of selfish sensual indulgences, then happiness will continue to elude us. Selfish, self-indulgences lead to pleasure AND pain, but not real happiness. However, if we are working long hours in selfless service to others, like the hungry and homeless, then in this case, we are certain to gain genuine happiness. Any noble pursuit will create real and lasting happiness.

We should also seek balance in our diet. For optimum health and happiness, we should avoid over-indulging in food or drink. Food can bring a measure of contentment, but not real happiness. Being drunk or high is a poor substitute for happiness. Getting drunk is a perfect example of a sensual indulgence that brings pleasure followed by pain and suffering. Real happiness can never be attained through the use of drugs or alcohol! We should also seek balance in our activities. Every day we should set aside time for exercise AND relaxation or meditation. We should avoid spending too much time at the gym or too much time in front of the TV. Balance is the key to a happy life!

Want more happiness in your life? Embrace Truth! This is absolutely essential. Happiness can only be attained, if we are seeking balance and harmony within ourselves. What does it mean to have balance within? It means there can be no conflict between what we think, what we say and what we do. We can't think one thing, and say another. We can't say one thing and do another. Inner conflicts are a real barrier to happiness. We must embrace truth even if it is scary, unpopular, embarrassing or even contrary to what we think is best for us. Living truth is always what's best for us. We cannot be happy while living a lie. It's bad enough when we lie to others. It's devastating to our happiness and well-being when we lie to ourselves.

If you really hate your job, quit! Life is too short to spend the majority of our time doing anything less that what we truly love doing. If you have a job, and a secret passion, quit your job and follow your passion. If you do what you love and it benefits others, then happiness will be yours.

If you are married and having an affair, confess! We cannot serve two masters! Affairs only bring short-term pleasure followed by long-term suffering! Embrace the truth, even if it might bring short-term suffering. Living Truth will eventually bring real happiness. If someone is controlling or abusive to you, tell them honestly how you feel. Don't lash out in anger—that will only cause you additional pain. We have to be honest with ourselves and others. However we must express our honesty with love and kindness to achieve balance, harmony and ultimately happiness. Only when our thoughts, words and deeds reflect truth, can we achieve real and lasting happiness.

Embracing Truth is also connected to our personal philosophy in life. If our own personal truth closely reflects Universal Truths, then real happiness is all but guaranteed! In the following chapter are examples of universal truths that we should embrace to achieve real and lasting happiness.

HAPPINESS IS

Happiness is knowing that God is pure and perfect Love.

Happiness is knowing that God Loves us and Forgives us unconditionally.

Happiness is knowing that God is ever present, ready and willing to offer us help and guidance.

Happiness is knowing that God is NOT angry, vengeful, wrathful or punishing.

Happiness is knowing that we are all one in God.

Happiness is knowing that our self-awareness is eternal and unending. We are Souls, and Souls are immortal.

Happiness is knowing that death is but an illusion.

Happiness is knowing that everyone who ever lived still lives! For God is the Father of the living, not the dead.

Happiness is knowing that our true home is in Paradise, or Heaven. Earth life is temporary and like college for Souls.

Happiness is knowing that all pain and suffering, trials and tribulations are temporary.

Happiness is knowing that suffering has a beneficial aspect, for it brings us closer to God by reducing our Karmic debt.

Happiness is knowing that life is fair, that there is divine justice in the world, for everyone gets exactly what's coming to them, whether it be pleasant or unpleasant.

Happiness is knowing that we will be reunited with our loved ones again and again, for true Love transcends time and space.

Happiness is knowing that we can NEVER be separate from our Heavenly Father, for He is the source of our existence.

Happiness is knowing that every person on earth is our spiritual Brother or Sister.

Happiness is knowing that we are not separate from Nature or Mother Earth.

Happiness is knowing that we are NOT our imperfect bodies.

Happiness is knowing that we are naturally evolving

towards perfection and enlightenment.

Happiness is knowing that we can find God existing within ourselves.

Happiness is knowing that with focused intention and a burning desire, we can manifest almost anything.

Happiness is knowing that we too can experience miracles.

Happiness is knowing that even though a leopard doesn't change its spots, people can change. Once we change our minds our actions are sure to follow.

Happiness is knowing that all men and women are created equal, and loved equally by God regardless of our apparent differences.

Happiness is knowing that guilt and self-punishment are entirely unnecessary.

Happiness is knowing that there is no hell or eternal damnation.

Happiness is knowing that we do not have to earn eternal life, for we ARE life eternal.

Happiness is knowing that Jesus still lives! And can be found by looking within.

CHAPTER 7

EVOLUTION

The Evolution of Form

One dictionary defines evolution as, "Growth, a process of continual change from a lower, simpler state to a higher, more complex state." The term, evolution, has become synonymous with the work of an English naturalist, Charles Darwin, and the 1859 publication of his book, *On the Origin of Species*. Terms like "natural selection" and "survival of the fittest" came out of this book. His theories are widely accepted by scientists today and are even taught in most public schools. However, there seems to be a debate over these theories and the Holy Bible's version of Creation. Personally, I don't see why both can't be true. God is the creator and source of ALL things in existence. And the fact that all forms are constantly changing for the better, evolving into perfection, implies divine architecture at work.

In my fifty years, I have witnessed quite a few Olympic games. It hasn't gone unnoticed by me that every year, we break existing world records. Man is always becoming stronger, faster and wiser, or more efficient. Some believe life happened spontaneously from the primordial soup. But does it make sense that life would not only survive and thrive, but continue to evolve towards perfection, if it was merely an accident? God created and animated all forms and is the force behind all change, growth and evolution.

THE EVOLUTION OF CONSCIOUSNESS

Our true nature is formless, eternal awareness. We are really just points of Light, immortal consciousness. We are perfect, just as our Heavenly Father is perfect. All His children are equally perfect and at the same time perfectly unique. No two souls have shared the same life experiences, so no two souls are identical. Our essence is identical and perfect, however, we appear different.

When our formless soul incarnates into the physical realm, it is encased in a vehicle of flesh and bone. The physical body is in turn a vehicle for our egos or personalities. Our egos are then vehicles for our behavioral tendencies, accumulated over many, many lifetimes. Ego, personality and character are all synonymous. Most women who have given birth to many children will tell you that all children are born with a complete personality, which remains fairly consistent throughout their lives. In each lifetime, we are refining our character. We adopt new tendencies and we drop some old ones. This is character development or the process of spiritual evolution. I realize that modern-day Christendom does not accept the truth of reincarnation. I tend to agree with Paramahansa Yogananda, the God realized yogi from India, who wrote in his autobiography, "The early Christian church accepted the doctrine of reincarnation, which was expounded by the Gnostics and by numerous church fathers, including Clement of Alexandria, the celebrated Origen (both third century) and St. Jerome (fifth century). The doctrine was first declared a heresy in

A.D. 553 by the second council of Constantinople. At that time, many Christians thought the doctrine of reincarnation afforded man too ample a stage of time and space to encourage him to strive for immediate salvation. But Truths suppressed lead disconcertingly to a host of errors. The millions have not utilized their "one lifetime" to seek God, but to enjoy this world, so uniquely won, to shortly be forever lost! The truth is that man reincarnates on earth until he has consciously regained his status as a son of God."

I believe that reincarnation is Truth, however, not a desired state. Teaching reincarnation is like having a class entitled, "How to flunk out of school."

Having to reincarnate is akin to being left back to repeat a grade because we were unable to learn what we needed to learn. It is not God's plan or desire that we should incarnate perpetually. He wants us to learn our lessons and graduate, transcend this world and evolve to the next, more challenging level of existence. Onward and upward, that is the plan. I understand why the church fathers wanted to abolish this doctrine. They knew that up until the time when Jesus descended into the flesh, all men were reincarnating, even the prophets. In the *Pistis Sophia*, Jesus is quoted as saying, "The Savior answered, saying to Mary, 'Amen, amen, I say to you: Before I came into the cosmos, no soul had entered into the Light .... I have turned Elijah around and directed him into the body of John the Baptizer, and the others I turned around, directing them into righteous bodies that will find the mysteries of the Light, ascend on high, and inherit the Light-Kingdom.'"

After He ascended back into heaven, salvation and ascension were now made available to all those who were ready to follow Jesus, both literally and figuratively. Figuratively, by using his life as an ideal to emulate, and literally, as in following the path he forged through the many levels of creation, through God's house of many mansion worlds. Each level requires a certain wisdom to proceed through the threshold gates. The sacred mysteries themselves are the keys necessary for ascension through these gates.

Now that the way was made ready, the church fathers wanted all men to seek salvation in this lifetime and not put it off until some future lifetime, which is why they abolished this doctrine. However, human nature is such that when most are told they have only one lifetime, instead of salvation, they choose instead to seek pleasure and fun. Just one lifetime? Let's party!!

When babies are born, that's when they are closest to their real natures. Babies are born with self-awareness, they know they exist and have perception, so they can perceive their environment. Awareness and perception are also synonymous. They go hand-in-hand. We can't have one without the other. To be aware is to perceive and to perceive is to be aware.

When a soul incarnates into the flesh, it acquires not only a body vehicle, but also a brain. The brain does not only regulate bodily functions, it also serves the purpose of cognition. Its job is to make sense out of what is being perceived. A newborn baby knows that it is perceiving something—it just doesn't know what. We have to be taught how to cognize the world around us. Cognition is the process of learning. We don't perceive the world as it really is, we instead see it as we were taught to see it. Since we are all taught to perceive it in the same way, we tend to think that we are all perceiving the same reality. However, a child raised in the city would certainly perceive a much different reality than a child raised in a tribe in the isolated regions of a rain forest. We each have our own unique perspective on the world around us. And although it seems as though we are all sharing one reality, in fact we are all creating our own reality. In whatever way we perceive the world, this *is* our reality, even if it's distorted by our judgments and our limited physical senses. Our philosophy, our beliefs, our personal paradigm *is* our reality. We believe what we see, because we see what we believe. We see what we expect to see. Everything we see must be integrated into our beliefs. If we don't believe it, we won't see it. To evolve spiritually, we must be open to new ideas, new experiences, new perspectives, and new beliefs. We must be open-minded to the Truths that our Father wishes to share with us.

As children grow, their conscious awareness continues to expand and evolve. Soon after learning to cognize the world around them, they develop the ability to re-cognize their surroundings. They develop memory, another function of consciousness. This aspect allows for the continued growth and evolution of awareness. The more we remember, the more we learn. Memory is essential for proper functioning in this physical realm. If we lose our ability to recognize our world, as is the case in Alzheimer's victims, we de-evolve back to a childlike state.

After we have learned to recognize the world around us, we then develop another aspect of consciousness. We now learn how to focus our awareness by developing attention. We know that children, when they are young, have incredibly short attention spans. Their ability to focus their awareness develops over time as they mature. As consciousness evolves, our ability to focus our attention increases. The advanced art of focused attention is called meditation or contemplation, another important aspect of consciousness needed for our spiritual evolution.

As children mature into adulthood, they are now capable

of perceiving their environment, capable of remembering that which they perceived and can focus their awareness on one thing or several. However, we have been taught to perceive a world of seemingly separate things, a world of opposites. We are taught to perceive the difference between right and wrong, fair and unfair, good and bad. We learn in and out, up and down, left and right, fast and slow, hot and cold, male and female, life and death, and on and on. This view of reality is called duality consciousness. We live in a world where every state has an opposite or dual nature. 99.9% of the world's population lives this reality. Many believe this to be the only reality. However, as we shall soon see, duality consciousness itself also has an opposite.

Those adults who choose to seek greater meaning in their lives by traversing the spiritual Path start by using their inherent powers of perception to become more aware of themselves. Instead of focusing all of their attention on the world outside of themselves, they begin to focus on what's happening within themselves instead. They begin to examine their own beliefs, motives and intentions. They observe their emotions, their thoughts, desires and habits. With continued practice, eventually they become aware of their unconscious re-actions to the world and to the people around them.

Self-consciousness (with a small "s") is the ability to recognize our own beliefs, intentions, desires and habits. It also entails a recognition of our personal faults and weaknesses. We see the parts of ourselves that need improvement. This particular aspect of consciousness evolution is by far the most difficult. It takes tremendous courage and fortitude to stare headlong into the mirror, while being witness to our own shortcomings. It's a totally gut-wrenching experience. I've heard this aspect being referred to as "the dark night of the soul." It's a very apt description, in my opinion. However for me, this period lasted several months. It was the most difficult and painful period of my life. Many can't stand the sight of their true characters being laid bare before them. At this point, usually one of three things happen. Firstly, some become overwhelmed and retreat into denial or unconsciousness. They have left the Path for now. Secondly, some become depressed or self-destructive or even suicidal—a sad state indeed. And thirdly, there are those who accept the truth about themselves, and choose to continue on the Path. They dig down deep within themselves and find the strength and courage to motivate themselves to engage in the process of self-correction. They take the necessary steps to eradicate selfish impulses and destructive behaviors. They seek truth in place of illusions. They replace false beliefs with real wisdom. At this point, they have entered the Path proper.

As our consciousness continues to evolve, at some point along the Path, we recognize our own inherent dual nature. We perceive ourselves as being part man, part God, part physical and part spiritual. A part of us is entirely selfish, while another part is giving and selfless. Part of us is observing the world outside of us and everyone in it, and another part of us is observing ourselves.

Observing ourselves? How does that work? Who is observing and who is being observed? We ask, who am I really? The one observing or the one being observed? This is a pivotal part of consciousness evolution, for when we identify ourselves with the observer within, our spiritual aspect, or God-selves, we now enter into Self-awareness with a capital "S". We are now ready to embrace real Truth, the Truth of who we really are. Only then, are we ready to evolve to the final phase of consciousness evolution, where we can perceive the one True Reality.

Unity consciousness is the highest expression of

consciousness and the opposite of duality consciousness. Unity consciousness is the one true reality. It's the state we all live in when not incarnated into the flesh, however, it can be accomplished and experienced here on earth. Those existing in Unity consciousness are considered enlightened souls. Enlightened beings can perceive oneness or Unity in a world of seemingly separate things. They perceive their inherent, unbroken connection to source or God. They know that they are not their bodies, but rather the consciousness that inhabits them. They know that they are not their egos or personalities. They know their egos are the vehicles of their earthly Karma and only exist while incarnated for the purpose of spiritual evolution. They recognize every soul on earth as their spiritual Brothers and Sisters, Sons and Daughters of our Father God. They can perceive duality as an illusion, a mere distortion of Unity. They recognize their inherent perfection, as unchanging, eternal consciousness, just like their Heavenly Father, perfect, unchanging and eternal.

THE EVOLUTION OF MAN

You may be asking yourself about now that if we are indeed perfect and unchanging, what then is evolving? You are probably saying to yourself that you don't feel perfect and you don't know anyone who is perfect either—right? What's evolving is our perceptions, our understanding of Truth. When we are incarnate into a physical body, within the illusion of duality consciousness, we perceive only imperfections and disconnectedness. While in between lifetimes, while in the heavenly realms, we experience Unity Consciousness and we then perceive perfection and connectedness. The slow process of enlightenment is learning how to perceive our inherent perfection and connection to Source while incarnate here on earth. This is why we are here. This is the meaning of life. We are here to "be" because we are life eternal, and to "become" perfect Sons and Daughters of God.

This process of perfection happens over many, many lifetimes. Since we are eternal in nature, time is not an issue. We are allowed to take as many lifetimes as we need to get it right. Our evolution proceeds with or without our understanding or awareness. It is happening naturally. However, once we become aware of this process, we can hasten it dramatically through self-effort. We can choose to go home sooner rather than later. It's completely up to us—free will remember? This then begs the question, if our evolution is happening naturally and we will all reach perfection eventually, then why would we want to work at it? The answer is quality of life. As long as we have to be here, shouldn't we want it to be the best experience possible? Wouldn't we rather live lives filled with understanding, peace and happiness, rather than endless pain and suffering? I'm sure given the choice, most would rather experience only love, peace and joy in their lives and that is exactly what is possible for us, if we choose to walk the spiritual Path in life. This Path to real and lasting Happiness is narrow and few find it—even fewer choose to traverse it. The path to pain and suffering is wide and many follow it.

Bill Murray's *Groundhog Day* is a movie that serves as a perfect metaphor for man's evolution. In the movie, Bill's character is an obnoxious, arrogant, self-centered TV weatherman sent to Punxsutawney, Pennsylvania, to see if Phil the groundhog sees his shadow. However, he has the bizarre experience of reliving the same day over and over again. At first he uses his foreknowledge of events to manipulate others for his own benefit. He seduces women, robs an armored truck, stuffs his face with pastries, skips work, drives through town like a maniac, and so on. No matter what he does, for him there are no consequences, because there is no tomorrow. After a while, he becomes despondent and depressed and eventually suicidal. He tries every way imaginable to kill himself in an attempt to end his nightmare, but every day he once again wakes up to another February 2nd Groundhog Day. Eventually he realizes that being self-indulgent doesn't make him happy and being self-destructive doesn't put an end to his suffering. So finally, he decides to try and use his foreknowledge of events to be of service to others. He catches a child who falls from a tree, he changes a tire on the side of the road for some elderly ladies. He gives a choking man the Heimlich maneuver and saves his life. He buys a ton of insurance from an old acquaintance and feeds a hungry homeless man. He performs good deeds all day long. This path leads him to real happiness, until he no longer cares if he relives the same day over and over. It's only at this point that he finally wakes up to the next day, February 3rd.

Imagine that every February 2nd that he experienced was equivalent to an entire lifetime. As long as we are selfish and self-indulgent, all our lifetimes will look and feel the same—endless pain and suffering. Only by opening our hearts, seeking to be of service to others, and engaging in acts of love and kindness do we experience spiritual growth and evolution. Only then do we move forward. Only then do we transcend suffering and experience life with real and lasting Happiness.

The Seven Energy Centers

Eastern medicine has a history of over five thousand years. Ancient Adepts were able to map out the subtle energy body of a human. It included seven major vortices along the spine called chakras, which drew into the body invisible life force energy or "chi." This chi energy is then spread throughout the body via pathways called meridians. Their understanding and philosophy was quite simple. If chi flows unobstructed throughout the body, a person has good health. If there are blockages of this vital energy, this was the root cause of pain and disease. They created healing modalities such as acupuncture and Reiki to remove these blockages and restore health and vitality. The seven chakras split white light into its seven major component colors similar to a rainbow. Each chakra uses one of these colors. A person's aura will reflect which chakra is most dominant. The dominant color of our auras will give us clues as to where we are in our evolution.

Energy Center # 1

This is called the root chakra. It is at the base of the spine and is our connection to Mother Earth. Its associated color is red. Those functioning primarily from this center are engaged in basic survival. They are trying to remain here, grounded to the earth. All children have red auras. The sick and dying have red auras and the homeless, as well.

Energy Center #2

This is the sacral or sexual chakra. It is located on the spine just below the navel. It's associated color is orange. Its energy feeds the sexual organs. Most teenagers have red and orange auras. Adults addicted to sex have orange auras. Anyone who spends the majority of their time and energy engaged in the pursuit of sexual expression, function from this energy center.

ENERGY CENTER #3

This is the solar plexus chakra. It is located in the midsection just above the navel. It's associated color is yellow. Its energy feeds the digestive organs. Anyone who spends the majority of their time and energy pursuing fame and fortune, power and influence function from this energy center. This is where the majority of adults are, evolutionarily speaking. This is the energy behind all selfish pursuits.

ENERGY CENTER #4

This is called the heart chakra. It is located around the center of the chest, and its associated color is green. Its energy feeds the heart and lungs. Anyone who spends the majority of their time and energy in selfless service to others, function from this energy center. This includes people such as doctors and nurses, those selflessly serving in the military, and volunteers. Only those functioning from this chakra and above have any chance at true happiness. Intention is the key here. If a man pursues the medical profession to make lots of money and earn respect and notoriety, then he is functioning from the solar plexus, not the heart. A man who joins the military because of a genuine desire to serve his country and protect his loved ones works from the heart.

ENERGY CENTER #5

This is called the throat chakra, for obvious reasons. Its associated color is light blue. Those functioning from this energy center are great singers, communicators, orators and speechmakers. However, once again, intention is the key.

Only those engaged in the spread of Truth and wisdom, like ministers, are truly functioning from here. Hitler was a great orator, however, his intention was the acquisition of power and influence—again we are back down to the solar plexus.

Energy Center #6

This is called the brow chakra. It is located directly between the eyebrows. Its associated color is dark blue or indigo. This energy is directly liked to the pineal gland and it is the center of psychic abilities. Those functioning from here use their psychic abilities for the benefit of others. Edgar Cayce is an obvious example. He did over fourteen thousand readings and never charged anyone a dime, even though he and his family struggled financially. The development of psychic abilities is a natural function of our evolution. Those functioning from here are highly evolved indeed.

Energy Center #7

This is called the crown chakra. It is located at the top of the head, and is directly linked to the master gland of the body, the pituitary. Its color is purple. Those enlightened souls living in Unity Consciousness are functioning from this energy center. These highly evolved souls are in direct connection with the Divine at all times. They are veritable angels walking the Earth. There are very few individuals functioning from this chakra. The Master Jesus is a great example.

What's evolving is our perception of ourselves. Once we perceive ourselves as perfect children of God, one with His Omnipresent Mind, then our evolution, our education is complete. We can stay here in a perfected state or move on to the next more challenging stage, the next level as it were. In God's infinite creation, there are always more levels, endless steps on the infinite Path to God. When we live our lives unaware of this process, it's like being a leaf stuck in an eddy, a whirlpool on the side of a river. Continuous movement and yet going nowhere. It's time to get unstuck and moving again down the river of Life Eternal. When we let the river take us, go with the flow as it were, we are effortlessly moving towards perfection, love and oneness. When we resist life, when we resist what is, it's like trying to swim against the current. We end up exhausted and going nowhere. Let go and let God guide us unto Him. It's inevitable, because of God's will for our continued growth, change and evolution, we are all doomed to perfection. Embrace change. Embrace growth. Embrace evolution. To embrace change, growth and evolution is to embrace God, our Father. Surrender to the marvelous changes He has in store for us. He knows exactly what is best for us and He wants what's best for us. We have to trust in that. We have to have faith in His Wisdom and Guidance. Change is growth. Growth is evolution and evolution is always forward and good. So change is good! Embrace change! Embrace your own evolution!

CHAPTER 8

RULES

What is a Universal Law? A Universal law is a natural law, which applies to every single evolving intelligent species in the entire physical cosmos. They are natural laws established by God, for the proper functioning of His creation. Although He is the ultimate Observer, ever present in the whole of creation, He does not judge. His rules were set into motion at the beginning of time, and continue to run perfectly, not unlike the parameters of a computer program. His rules keep the Universe in balance. His rules make sure everyone evolves to perfection, according to His plan. His rules guarantee fairness and equal opportunity to all. When understood properly, the rules of creation can be used to change our lives for the better. We can use our new understanding to overcome all suffering. We can use them to our advantage to hasten our evolution and experience life on earth with abundant Love, Peace and Happiness. They can be applied to our lives in such a way as to overcome the illusion of duality consciousness and achieve Unity or oneness with God. Through them we can even achieve heaven on earth, and eventually ascend to the heavenly realms, to be one with our Father forever. However, a misunderstanding of universal law is in my opinion, the leading root cause of our endless suffering. Our misunderstanding of his natural laws is also the reason we have become convinced of the illusion that God can be angry, vengeful and punishing.

LIFE IS SIMILAR TO A VIDEO GAME

It's a little embarrassing to admit this, but I remember the very first video game. Do you remember Atari's Pong? Video ping pong. It was very simple indeed. A single screen with a dividing line down the middle, two paddles that only moved up or down, one for each player, and a little white blip or ping pong ball bouncing off the edges of the screen. And as simple as it was, it was still fun. We had no idea just how popular and complex video games would become in the future. It was a marvelous thing to witness over the years. Its mind-boggling to think that today we can play a video game against an opponent who is living on the other side of the world in real time. They have certainly come a long way in a very short period of time.

In addition to being a good source of entertainment, video simulators are now being used to train individuals with high-risk jobs, like pilots. Training simulations save time and money. It's certainly safer and less expensive for pilots in training to make their mistakes in a simulator—right?

Generally speaking, what would be the purpose within a video game? I would suggest that the purpose is to win the game by overcoming a series of obstacles through trial and error. After overcoming either obstacles or our opponent, we win entrance to the next more challenging level or we win the game outright. Either way, the purpose is to win. Life itself is not unlike this. We each experience a series of incarnations, each fraught with challenges and obstacles. Through the process of trial and error, we figure out the rules of the game to overcome all obstacles and win entrance into the next more challenging level. Ultimately we win entrance into the Kingdom of Heaven.

We are, all of us, subject to the same rules or Universal Laws. Because of this, there is absolute fairness built into the system. If we break a rule, we suffer equally. Live within the rules and we all benefit equally. God is like a good government, He promotes equality, fairness and unity. We are, all of us, engaged in the process of evolution either by choice or by natural impulse. Evolution is a natural process, built into the system. It's happening with or without our awareness. However, if we are aware of the system and its rules, we can choose to live within the framework of Universal Law and make the rules work for us, thereby allowing us to overcome all pain and suffering in life. If we continue to break the rules out of ignorance, our natural evolutionary course will be long and painful indeed.

Have you ever given much thought as to how a video game is constructed? Today's games are so complex! We are given so many choices. We can sometimes move in any direction for quite some distance. But that distance is always limited. At some point, we reach the edge, the outside parameters of the game. For the parameters of each game *are* limited—not unlike life here and now. We also live within certain parameters. We cannot live under the water like so many fishes. We don't fly in the air like the birds. We don't live within the earth like bugs or bats. We live on top of the earth like other mammals. We were designed to walk upon the earth. This is one of our parameters. Within the game's parameters, we can choose to interact with many different things. We choose the obstacles to overcome, for the most part. Sometimes we are given so many choices, it feels as though we have free will within the game, right? How does the game know what we are going to do next and respond to it appropriately? It almost feels like an intelligence within the game responding to us, doesn't it? But we know that's not the case. The architect of the game is not inside of it, judging us and responding emotionally to our choices—right? The architect of the game had to calculate in advance, every possible action we could undertake, and write a program to respond to it appropriately.

Every possible action we can choose is accounted for, and an automatic response is built into the game. There are no surprises in a video game. Every action we take will initiate the very same reaction. This is exactly how we learn how to overcome the obstacles. By learning the game's automatic responses. Every action is designed to either be a help or a hindrance. Points are won or taken away. Life is extended or cut short.

The universal laws that govern us work exactly the same way. Every interaction we have with another person will either bring us happiness or cause us to suffer. Every interaction with another will either advance our growth and evolution or stunt it. The automatic responses built into the system are identical for each and every person—there are no favorites. If we work within the system, our rewards are the same. If we break the rules, our pain and suffering is exactly the same. Just like a video game. Responses are consistent and fair. And every video game is designed with a way to win. So too with life. If we learn the law and live within the rules and learn to overcome all obstacles, we will eventually win the game, win entrance into His eternal Kingdom.

There was one particular video game that I enjoyed very

much—maybe a little *too* much. I became obsessed, spending an inordinate amount of time and energy trying to win this game. I think it was the only game I completely mastered. The game was Mike Tyson's Punch-Out. Boxing, I love it! As a kid I learned judo and karate. I've always enjoyed the martial arts. I took tremendous pride in my virtual victory over the man himself, Mike Tyson. However, to get to him, I first had to beat two dozen other fighters, each with elevated skill sets over the previous. Each had a unique style, which I had to learn to overcome. Early on I learned something very interesting. If I went into a bout very aggressively, with fists flailing, I was sure to get knocked out fairly quickly. However, if I waited patiently for my opponent to make the first move, countered with a block and then became more aggressive, I was ultimately victorious. This simple method allowed me to win the entire game.

I've discovered that the same trick applies to life in general. I've learned that it is not so much our actions that carry the most weight in life, but our re-actions. Do you believe that you have free will? What is free will? Does it mean we can make any choice in life we want? Does it mean that we are in control of our lives? Are you in control of your life? Do you get up each morning and plan your day? Does your day always unfold according to your plans? Not usually, right? We don't have control of the weather. We can't keep a tornado from ripping our house apart. We can't keep the drunk driver from crashing into the back of us—right? We can't keep our boss from firing us. We can't stop others from gossiping about us. We can't keep our partner from cheating on us or walking out on us—right? The truth is, we have zero control over what happens to us on a daily basis, however, we do have complete control over how we re-act to whatever happens to us. This is free will. We always choose how we respond to life. The proper re-action to life's events is how we win the game. The proper reaction to events is how we overcome, it's how we attain real Peace. Our reactions are our choice always, and in all ways. We choose between anxiety or peace, anger or forgiveness, sadness or joy, fear or love. These choices determine whether or not we win in the game of life. We are all given free will to choose for ourselves.

Many Masters have come and gone throughout history, leaving behind their accumulated wisdom as a roadmap for the rest of us. Since they were successful at overcoming life's challenges and illusions, we too have the same potential to follow in their footsteps, and achieve success as they have. I'm reminded of a quote from Jesus in the New Testament, "I tell you the Truth, anyone who has faith in me, will do what I have been doing. And he will do even greater things than these." (John 14:12)

He certainly inspired me to want to be more like Him, to reach for the stars, to be the best that I can possibly be, to fulfill my highest potential. Reaching that goal is not easy. It requires commitment and sacrifice, not to mention lots of study and hard work. No real progress can be made, however, until we become acquainted with the rules of the road, the universal laws governing physical existence. Learning them is fairly easy, compared with actually integrating them into our lives and living them completely. Once they are applied to our lives, we can accomplish anything! Once we start living within the framework of Truth, life is a completely different experience. A life lived in ignorance of these laws is fraught with pain and suffering, endless obstacles and challenges. A life lived in harmony with universal laws is filled to the brim with Peace, Love and Happiness. The choice is ours. We have been given free will to either serve God and our fellow man or to serve ourselves, to live within the law or outside of it. My hope is that we all choose wisely.

LAW OF CYCLES

Anyone who spends some time observing Nature, will eventually perceive the law of cycles playing out in the physical universe. It's quite easy to spot. Most are familiar with the life cycle. Birth, life and death. Rebirth, life and death. Again and again. Within nature, we see flowers grow and bloom, shrivel and die and disappear, just to reappear, grow and die again the following year. Animals are born, grow to adulthood, procreate, grow old and die. Their young do the same, and life continues. Every year, we cycle through the seasons of winter, spring, summer and fall again and again. Leaves on the trees bloom in the spring, flower in the summer and shrivel and drop in the fall. In winter, the trees look dead. But we know that life will emerge once again come spring. We know that their seeming death is but an illusion.

Let's look at time. Time is nothing more than the observed cycles of planets and stars. One day is a complete cycle of the earth on its axis. One month is a complete lunar cycle. One year is a cycle of the earth around our sun. A decade is a cycle of ten years and a century is a cycle of one hundred years. A millennium is a cycle of a thousand years and one grand solar cycle is one cycle of our sun through all twelve houses of the zodiac. This particular cycle is called the precession of the equinox and is almost 26,000 years in length. The end of that cycle is to be concluded on December 21, 2012.

We can see that time is a construct based on the

movement of the planets and stars. What if there were no stars and planets? Time could not exist, right? Time is based on relative movement. In this vast universe, everything seems to be moving relative to everything else. Imagine floating in outer space. Imagine all the stars disappearing. Without something else with which to orient yourself, direction becomes meaningless. Up down ,left, right, forward and backward, here and there—they all have lost their relative meaning. So too has movement. Unless you have something to move towards or away from, movement and speed become irrelevant. Unless there are stars whizzing past your spaceship window, there is no way to know if you are moving or not. Five miles an hour and five million miles per hour would look and feel exactly the same. Time too becomes meaningless. Without moving planets to track, there is no way to mark the passing of time. Instead we have eternal duration, the omnipresent, ever unfolding present moment, or now. The ancient Hindus believed that the entire physical creation itself is cyclical. They believe that God breathes out the expanding universe and all life therein. Trillions of years later He breathes creation back into himself, for an extremely long period of non-existence—no planets, no stars, no people—just God. Then once again in an unending cycle, He breathes out creation and all life to evolve once again. The entire physical universe is created with perfection, cycles within cycles within cycles. Albert Einstein, when observing the perfection of the universe, likened it to a pocket watch. Perfect order and balance, intelligently designed, everything intimately connected to everything else, like the interconnected cogs of a complex timepiece. He perceived order and balance in the universe. He knew logically that there had to be a intelligent and powerful architect at work behind the scenes. He spent his life in the pursuit of the ultimate mathematical equation, one that would explain the mysterious balance of forces in existence like the weak force, the strong force, electromagnetism and gravity. Scientists today are still working on this equation.

If we spend some time and look closely at the nature of Nature, we can perceive the Truth in the cyclical nature of existence. There is Truth in the concept of re-incarnation. Our eternal souls enjoy endless lifetimes within this physical universe for the purpose of just being, and for the purpose of perfecting our characters. Spiritual evolution. Our essence, our souls are eternal, perfect and unchanging.

Law of Attraction

Early on in my massage career, while working at a rehabilitation clinic, I met a patient whose story touched me deeply. The majority of my patients were automobile accident victims. I usually treated them three times a week for many months. Over the months, some become comfortable with me and shared their life stories. This man whom I will call John, was truly a tortured soul, his life was endless agony, both physically and emotionally. He confessed to me that he was convinced that God hated him. I was treating his wounds from a car crash. As it turned out, it was the seventh major accident he has had in only four years! I was thinking to myself that this guy is probably the worst driver imaginable, however, he made a comment that most times he was sitting motionless at a light when someone else slammed into him. He felt there was a big target painted on his back. It bothered me deeply that he thought that God hated him—I just knew that wasn't possible. I felt there must be a reason for his incredible string of bad luck, other than God's wrath. So I dug a little deeper. I asked him if anything traumatic happened in his life prior to all those accidents. Tears began to well up in his eyes, as he told me the most tragic tale ever. Apparently, his neighbor had stopped by a bar on the way from work and had too much to drink. He was only a block from home when he ran over and killed John's little girl, who was playing in the street in front of her house. He said he could never get that gory scene out of his head. He admitted that since that time, he had become obsessed with thoughts of anger and vengeance. He fantasized constantly about running this guy over with his car. His tale was disturbing to me. I prayed to God for understanding. I felt a strong desire to help this man or at least have some understanding as to why life can seem so unfair. I had never met anyone who was suffering so much. On the surface, it seemed as though he had every right to perceive his reality as he did. However, I could not help bit feel that he was suffering from a misunderstanding. Eventually I gained some wisdom into the law of attraction. I shared my wisdom with John in an effort to reduce his suffering. I share it with you now for the same reason.

If we wish to move in a particular direction, we give a command to our brains, which in turn commands our bodies to move. Whatever we desire, we have the power to move towards—correct? Well, we also possess the power to magnetize the objects of our desire, and have them start moving towards us. We attract people, objects and experiences into our lives simply by focusing our attention and intention on those objects. How? Do you not know ye are Gods? The omnipresent mind of God exists within us. We are always tapped into it, whether we are conscious of it or not. Whatever we desire, we manifest, intentionally or unintentionally. We are constantly using the omnipotent power of the indwelling Lord to magnetize or attract into our lives EVERYTHING we focus our thoughts on and add emotion to.

The thoughts themselves are like rockets, and the fuel or the energy behind their manifestation comes from emotion, like intense desire. The greater the desire, the faster the manifestation. I'm sure you've heard the expression, "Be careful what you ask for, because you might just get it." This is a truth in the law of attraction. We always manifest what we desire, even if what we desire is not in our best interest! My massage teacher, Dale, would say, "What you resist persists." This makes sense in the light of this truth. If we focus a lot of thought on our fears, and then add emotion to that fear, we are only helping to manifest more of what's frightening to us! Truth is, the predominating thoughts in our minds are being made manifest, whether we know it or not. We help to create our own reality, knowingly or unknowingly. The law of attraction is universal in nature. It applies to every intelligent evolving entity in the physical universe. Simply put, whatever we think about most often will surely come to pass.

In John's case, his obsessive preoccupation with thoughts of violence with an automobile were being made manifest in his life over and over again. And the events were proportional to the depth of his emotion. Seven major accidents in four years!? I explained to John that for him to achieve some peace, he would have to practice forgiveness and stop thinking violent thoughts. That's why Jesus said to "Do unto others as you would have them do unto you." The golden rule—for verily, according to the law of attraction, whatever you wish for others, you also attract to yourself. To have peace, we have to "bless those that curse us," for we are sure to receive that blessing. We have to desire only goodness or "thirst for His Righteousness." Only when we can love ourselves and love others as ourselves, can we know peace, love and happiness.

Those outside of us are not really separate from us. We are all one in God. Think ill of no one, curse no one, never refuse a call for help, and never pass up an opportunity to practice love and kindness, mercy and compassion. If our intention is to experience God's presence, then with focused thoughts and a burning desire, He will reveal Himself to us. The law of attraction guarantees this! If we focus our desires on Love, we will find it. If we focus our desires on peace, we will attain it. If we focus our desire on physical health and well-being, we shall be healed. If we focus our thoughts on our illnesses, they will persist. If we focus on our poverty, it will persist. If we focus on being in competition with someone else, someone else will constantly be in competition with us. If we focus on acquiring wealth, abundance and security, we will achieve it. Whatever we expect to receive, we do receive. If we expect miracles, we will experience miracles. If we expect bad luck, we receive bad luck. Jesus promises us that whatever we ask for in His name, and *expect* to receive, we shall receive. Faith is an emotion that fuels manifestation. Faith-backed sincere prayers are quickly manifested. Whatever the mind of man can conceive and *believe,* it can achieve.

We are once again faced with a choice, free will to either manifest sensual pleasures and monetary wealth along with the inevitable effects of pain and suffering or we can manifest real and lasting happiness and inner peace by being obedient to God's universal laws. God our Father loves us so much he has given us free will, the power to choose for ourselves.

He loves us so much He uses his infinite power to assist us in experiencing whatever dream takes hold in our minds. He does not discriminate or judge our choices—instead, He happily fulfills EVERY desire born within. So it's up to us to discriminate, to choose with wisdom, the kind of future we wish to live. If we choose to live in fear, we are guaranteed to experience more fear. If we instead choose to live in Faith, we are guaranteed to experience His Peace. If we insist that God doesn't exist, we will not experience His presence. We perceive what we expect to perceive. Every thought born within our minds is heard by the omnipresent Spirit within us and is acted upon through the natural law of attraction. In this sense, all thought is prayer. Formal spoken prayer is useful but not necessary. God knows our minds, He knows what we want. It is absolutely essential that we accept these truths and start monitoring our thoughts. Knowledge is power. Use the power inherent in the knowledge of the workings of the law of attraction to literally change your life.

Tend your mind as you would a garden. Plant only positive uplifting thoughts and nourish them with emotions of love and faith. Tend your garden daily, for a garden left unattended will surely sprout weeds or negative, self-destructive thoughts. Without the sufficient nourishment of faith, the weeds are watered with the tears of bitterness, made to grow and expand with the emotion of doubt, until they overtake the garden and choke out anything useful, productive and positive.

We must assume responsibility for our lives. We must accept the truth that we are helping to co-create our lives, both with our fears and our dreams. Whichever we focus on, we manifest. We must be more vigilant, more conscious of our thoughts. We must practice prayer, visualization and positive affirmations. They are all effective methods for actively, consciously using the law of attraction to create a better life. We can help to create a better future for ourselves by simply visualizing a better future. Collectively, we as humanity can help create a better future by imagining one, collectively. If we all *expect* a catastrophe in December of 2012, then we are certainly capable of manifesting one. However, if we collectively ask for and *expect* a loving peaceful transition into the new age, we are equally capable of experiencing that as well. God our Father wants for us whatever we want for ourselves. We just have to choose. I've made my choice. What do you want? For those who wish to know God, a persistent sincere desire is a good start. If you fan the flames of desire into a raging fire of passion, God will surely reveal Himself to you. You are then on your way to experiencing real and lasting Happiness, Love, and Peace.

LAW OF BALANCE

The law of balance is by far the most recognizable of all natural laws. It should be, for it is the most comprehensive and integrated of all Universal Laws. Science recognizes the truth inherent in universal balance. Do you remember your high school physics class. Do you remember Newton's third law of motion? It states that for every action or force in nature, there is an equal and opposite reaction—equal and opposite like a balanced mathematical equation—*perfectly* balanced. The laws of motion can be easily understood using billiard balls as an example, matter colliding with other matter or, in this case, billiard balls. With a rudimentary understanding of the laws of physics, we can learn to predict chain reactions by calculating momentum, velocity, spin and angular deflections. Because reactions to force are always equal and opposite and therefore *predictable*, we can easily sink one billiard ball after another.

Is it really such a stretch to imagine that if there does indeed exist a verifiable, scientific natural law of action and reaction, cause and effect, for all inanimate matter like billiard balls, then there also exists a natural law in effect for all animated matter like people? Sounds logical doesn't it? It was recognized by the ancient Adepts and their wisdom was passed down through the Hindu and Buddhist religions. They call it Karma. The law of cause and effect, action and re-action. There are many teachings about this Universal law, such as we reap what we sow, what goes around comes around, do unto others as you would have them do unto you, you get out of it just what you put into it, keep that up and you'll get what's coming to you, or keep going in that direction and you'll wind up where you're headed. Jesus recommended that we do unto others as you would have them do unto you, because He knew the law of balance that unerringly ensures that whatever you do to others, others *will* do to you! If we love others, others will love us. If we lie, steal and cheat others, others will lie, cheat and steal from us. If we give abundantly to others, the Universe will bring us abundance. We receive exactly what we give—equal and opposite—balanced. Every exchange we have with another person is an exchange of energy. That exchange has to be balanced out, somehow, someway, sometime. This is why reincarnation is essential to the proper functioning of God's perfect laws. Not all interchanges can be balanced out in one lifetime. We are always being reborn alongside people from our past. The Universe is giving us endless opportunities to balance out our Karma, work out issues from the past and reunite with lost loves.

As I said, all exchanges are energetic in nature. We either give something, take something or receive something in every exchange we have with another person. If we give something to someone, the universe makes sure that we receive something in the future of equal value. In essence, we have earned a universal credit. It's money in the bank in a manner of speaking or what Jesus referred to as "Treasures in Heaven." If we take something from someone, we have earned the equivalent of a Universal Debit. You now owe the Universe. If we develop the habit of taking from others, say like in the case of a professional thief, then the universe comes calling to collect that debt. How do we pay off our debts to the Universe? We pay it off by experiencing pain and suffering. Every unfortunate and painful thing that has ever happened to us throughout our lives, is a direct result of the Universal law of balance acting upon us. Our bad luck is nothing more than the universe balancing out an equation, paying off a debt. We get exactly what's coming to us, no more, no less. The law is perfectly fair and balanced. There really is no such thing as luck or coincidence. Everything that happens to us is the law of balance in action. "Vengeance is mine sayeth the Lord." Why? Because He is vengeful? No, because He has established a law, which makes sure everyone gets exactly what's coming to them. There is no need for us to be angry or act out violently. He has taken care of it. Retribution would only cause us additional suffering. That's why forgiveness is so important. It's the only proper response to transgressions. It's the only one that doesn't cause us any further suffering. Because forgiveness is a genuine act of love and kindness, it instead has the effect of Happiness. All acts of revenge will only cause additional debt to the Universe and ultimately more suffering.

If we allow ourselves to passively receive something in an exchange with another, we do not create Karmic debt. Receiving is energetically neutral. Whether we receive from our family and friends or from the Universe directly, we can receive abundance without incurring debt. Taking is bad, receiving is good. Giving is better. Giving is the only way to pay off our debts to the universe and ultimately win the game of life. Giving is how we create real Happiness. Giving and happiness go hand-in-hand. To give is to know happiness, to be happy is to know how to give. We can reach the gates of heaven once we evolve to the heart center and learn to give with an open heart. We can pass through the gates once we pay off our Karmic debts by giving more to the world than we take from it. We are here to become like our perfect Father, giving, loving and forgiving.

What is destiny? Destiny is our near future mapped out for us by the law of balance. Every cause must have an effect. Every action must have a reaction. Everything we experience in life is a consequence of our past actions, good and bad. Everything that happens to us is an effect. Something we did in the past is the cause. It is simply incorrect to think that somehow others are to blame for our suffering or that God is punishing us. He is not mad at us. He loves us and forgives us unconditionally. His program is running perfectly, unerringly. Life may appear to be unfair at times, however, from the big picture perspective, life is very fair, fair and balanced. Once we figure out the rules governing us, balance out all equations and fulfill our destiny in accordance with His will, then we can go home to Him.

The Karmic Quotient

Did you know that every single consumer in the United States has a credit score? There are three major companies whose purpose it is to collect financial data and create profiles on each of us. They look closely at our debts, our available credit, our payment history, and any other relevant information they can gather. They then feed all this data into their computer programs, programs created by bankers, representing their ideas of what's good and what's bad. The number that the program computes is our credit score. This number is constantly being recomputed as new information becomes available. This number gives lenders a clue as to where we stack up against other consumers. We are graded in other words. This grade, this credit score, is what lenders use as a guide to decide whether or not to lend us any money and at what percentage interest rate. When we go to borrow money from a bank for a credit card, a car or a home mortgage, this number can affect the nature of this process quite dramatically. The point I'm making is this—we have a number and it is affecting our lives, whether we are aware of it or not. Our choices determine the number. If we choose poorly, our number will go down, but if we choose wisely, we can improve our credit score.

There is another number affecting all of our lives, and every soul on earth has one. This number is directly associated with the law of balance. It's called the "Karmic Quotient." This number is affecting all of our lives, 24-7. Only because the law of balance does this, also. It's essential we understand the basic functioning of this Universal law. The Quotient is calculated thus:

(All Positive thoughts, words and deeds)
+
(All Negative thoughts, words and deeds)

Universal Laws of God = **KQ**

All positive thoughts, words and deeds, plus all negative thoughts, words and deeds, divided into God's Universal Laws equals our **K**armic **Q**uotient. In this equation, it is God who is deciding what is good and what is bad, what is useful and helpful, versus what is wasteful and destructive. His laws are absolutely fair, equally applied to all people. Our credit score only takes into account our financial habits. Our Karmic Quotient takes into account every habit, every thought, every word spoken every action undertaken. It is precise, accurate and fair. This number has everything to do with our quality of life. And even though we can never know the complexities and intricacies of the law, we can have an understanding of it from a larger perspective, the big picture, if you will.

Just like within a video game, or a computer program, every action we choose has a built-in response. Some actions add points to our total, while some take points away. Same thing in life—every action we undertake already has a numeric value attached to it. It's not important to know the exact numbers involved. We only have to realize that every action will have either or positive or negative effect upon our total score. Earlier we discussed energy exchanges. Every time we have an exchange with another person, we affect our score. If we give something, we earn a credit, and our Karmic debt is reduced. If we instead take something in that exchange, we earn a debit, and our Karmic debt has increased. If we allow ourselves to passively receive with an open heart, our score goes unchanged. We can even receive incredible abundance and wealth, and NOT incur any Karmic debt. Taking is bad, receiving is good, and giving is better.

Incarnation is required of any soul with a negative KQ. This is the law. Even the tiniest amount necessitates incarnation. I like to believe that SIDS, sudden infant death syndrome, is an example of souls that have fulfilled their Karmic obligations just from the trauma and suffering of birth. They are then free to ascend to the Heavenly realms. Every soul born on earth has a negative KQ, and is working off past life debts, even children. This is why they are made to suffer here, as much as anyone else. Karmic debts explain why "innocent" children experience pain and suffering. I also like to believe that children who pass away before their time, have simply fulfilled their Karmic obligations and are free to leave, free to ascend to their Father.

How do we know what our number is? It's not possible to know our number, however, it's important to know that it exists, that it is affecting our lives and can be changed. Knowing how to improve it is far more important than knowing what the number is.

If we are predators, always looking to take from the world, then our negative Karmic Quotient is steadily increasing. In the future, our destiny will be filled with lots of pain and suffering. We will experience only bad luck. We will always be in the wrong place at the wrong time. Nothing goes our way. It feels as though the universe is taking a dump on us constantly. We become convinced that we are cursed and that God hates us. We feel as if we are being punished. If our negative KQ increases steadily, our lives will eventually feel like Murphy's Law on steroids. If it can go wrong, it will, and at the worst possible moment. Does this sound familiar? Have I just described your life? Good, then keep reading because this book is being written with you in mind.

If we have a small negative quotient, then our lives are pleasant for the most part, perhaps even boring. Not much drama. Not very much pain and suffering. Just the occasional tribulations, some good luck mixed with bad luck. All in all, a pretty normal life.

If we work off all our debts and begin cultivating a positive KQ, then our lives are filled with blessings. We are always in the right place at the right time, only good things come to us, we experience lives with abundant peace, love and joy.

If we develop a large positive quotient, then we become as veritable angels walking the Earth. We can extend blessings to others, we can heal others, and we can easily manifest anything we desire. We become agents of the Lord, helping Him to do His work here on earth. We live in a state of endless Bliss, regardless of exterior circumstances.

All enlightened souls have a positive KQ. Only those souls with a positive KQ are capable of ascension. Once we have paid off our Karmic debts, we are free to ascend to Heaven forever, without having to reincarnate.

Once we decide which category we are in, then what? What do we do about it? There are only three things we can do. Firstly, if we don't know we have a number, or we don't care that we have a number, then we ignore it, do nothing. However, if we choose to do nothing, the Universe has no choice but to step in and make you pay your debts. How? By causing us pain and suffering. The force behind the law of balance is the force behind our suffering. Our choices are the ultimate cause of our suffering, however, it's the power and force behind the law that brings it about. The larger our number, the greater our pain and suffering. All actions must be balanced out, made equal and opposite. All causes reap effects, all actions beget re-actions. It's the law. We cannot avoid it. We cannot escape, or avoid paying our debts to the Universe.

There are those with very large negative quotients, who choose to end their suffering through suicide. Please know that this will fix nothing! The law will guarantee that they incarnate again quickly just to face the very same challenges that face them today. They have only succeeded in putting off the inevitable. We cannot escape our debts, even in death. Then there are those who feel as if they are already destined to go to hell, so they just continue to act in evil ways. Please know that there is no ultimate judgment or eternal damnation. Every evil action will reap further suffering and endless reincarnations. Those souls who continue to embrace evil actions will eventually live lives of endless pain and suffering. They will find themselves incarnated in parts of the world with abundant poverty and disease. Their debts must be paid.

Secondly, we can choose to engage in self-correction or spiritual growth. If we daily engage in doing good deeds for others, practice love and kindness, mercy and compassion, then the universe will *not* fill our destiny with pain and suffering. We are then allowed to pay off our debt in our own way, in our own time. Through selfless giving, we can overcome our negative KQ and the suffering it brings. Through the practice of Love, we pay off our debts and reduce our Karmic Quotient to zero, enabling us to break our earthly bonds and ascend forever into Heaven with our Father. Through love in action, we experience lives enriched with real and lasting Happiness.

There is also a third choice. It's the best and most appropriate, and the one I recommend to you. Whether we have a small or large negative Karmic Quotient, we can choose to surrender to God and ask for His Forgiveness. If this is done correctly, He may choose in His infinite Grace to forgive your trespasses, your transgressions, your sins, your Karmic debt. He is the all powerful Lord of the Universe. He is the creator of Universal law, He is not subject to them, and He can choose to override it, if He so chooses. Do this and your life can change as dramatically as did mine. I went from Murphy's Law on steroids to endless peace, love and joy—literally overnight. If it happened to me, it can happen to you. But once again, we are dealing with free will. It's entirely up to us to choose which path to follow. I recommend Door Number Three.

Once we come to accept the truths inherent in the law of balance, we can then use this knowledge and wisdom to change our lives for the better. We now possess the keys to our freedom. We need only to apply it with faith. First we realize that our life experiences are not random, but rather effects from our previous choices, then we need only make better choices today and those choices will reap better effects in the future.

Secondly, we should also realize that re-acting negatively to any person or event will only cause additional suffering for us in the future. That's why Jesus promoted loving and forgiving our enemies. He offered up a prayer of forgiveness for those who were in the moment nailing Him to a cross.

Thirdly we see that life is fair—everyone gets exactly what's due to them, positive or negative. We should now understand that God is only Loving and Forgiving. He is not and never has been angry, vengeful, wrathful or punishing. If we lose our fear of God, perhaps we will seek him out and ask for His amazing Grace, His Love and Forgiveness.

And lastly, we should now understand just how to go about finding real peace and lasting happiness in our lives, here and now. With this wisdom, we can become the true architects of our lives. We can overcome all obstacles, all suffering. Learn to live within the Universal laws of God, and we will experience perfect harmony with the Universe and everyone in it. Start today to sow future seeds of happiness. Give abundantly, love unconditionally and forgive everyone and everything!

LAW OF ONE

The law of one is the least understood and most abstract of all Universal laws of God. To even begin to have an understanding of it, we first need to remove from our minds the concept of impossible. Because with God all things are possible. In truth, we as children of an all-powerful, all-knowing Father God are really without limitations. The only limitations that exist for us are the ones we create for ourselves. Throughout history there have been many examples of things thought to be impossible, which were eventually rendered possible. If we *believe* we are limited, then we *are* limited. Once we experience the presence of God, all fear falls away, all limiting thoughts fade away, and in that space, we are capable of experiencing miracles or the seemingly impossible. Those with very high positive Karmic Quotients like Jesus, Buddha and Krishna used their understanding of the law of one to perform their many miracles. It's only from the perspective of unenlightened masses that their actions were viewed as miraculous or magical. There was absolutely nothing unnatural about their miracles. They were capable through an understanding and application of a Universal law, a natural law, the law of one. Do you wish you could perform miracles as Jesus did? I believe we can!

"I tell you the truth, anyone who has faith in me will do what I have been doing, and he will do even greater things than these." (John 14:12) Anyone can perform miracles with an understanding of the law of one. The deeper our connection with our Father, the greater our abilities. The more we engage in our spiritual growth and evolution, the greater our abilities. The lower our Karmic debt, or having a small negative KQ, the greater our abilities. The more we love our Heavenly Father and serve our fellow man, the greater our abilities to manifest and perform miracles or rather, the greater our chances that our prayers will be answered in a miraculous fashion. All desires and prayers are fulfilled eventually. The higher the negative KQ, the slower the process happens. The opposite is also true—the higher the positive KQ, the faster the manifestations occur. Jesus obviously displayed an intimate understanding of all the laws of God. When I first read the gospels, I was amazed at the consistency of his words and actions. He lived Truth. However, my friend, Irek, was a little confused by His actions with the poor little fig tree. Irek felt these actions were inconsistent with his understanding of a Master. Jesus wanted a fig, but this little bush bore no fruit, so He cursed it and it shriveled up on the spot. Irek couldn't help wonder why He didn't just bless the tree, have it bear fruit and enjoy a fig. After all He had manifested bread and fish for thousands, right? He obviously possessed the manifesting capabilities.

I asked the opinion of one of my clients, Reverend Tommy. He felt Jesus was giving His disciples a lesson on the power of the spoken word, the power to bless or the power to curse. This served as a soothing balm for a time, but something still didn't add up for me. I continued to ponder it until the Truth was revealed to me. I realized that all of Jesus' other miracles were desires manifested for the benefit of others. They were all selfless desires. The right kind of desire according to the Buddha. His desire for a fig was a selfish desire. Had He manifested a fig for himself He would have misused natural law and created negative Karma through the act of taking. Jesus was all about living a faultless life, demonstrating a life lived in perfect harmony with all God's laws. He broke no laws, created no negative Karma, ever! To react negatively to someone else's actions is to create negative Karma or Karmic debt. To forgive those who were in the moment nailing Him to a cross was to demonstrate to us all just how to earn "treasures in heaven." Jesus gave us an example of a life lived in perfect harmony with God and His Universal laws. Buddha in His wisdom gave us the tools necessary to become perfected masters of life. And the divine Krishna gave us a better understanding of the nature of God, and our connection to Him and the Universe and to each other. We are all one in God.

Understand that the law of balance is the force behind all suffering, while the law of one is the force behind all miracles. If we have a negative KQ, the law will make our lives miserable. We will feel oppressed, unlucky and cursed. If we develop a positive KQ, then the law will make our lives comfortable and pleasant. We are made to feel supported, lucky and blessed. We are capable then of manifesting our desires with ease, and living any experience we choose. Heaven and hell, exist together, here and now, in the physical plane as a consequence of the law of balance. Every thought we think, every word we speak every action we undertake will pave the way to either a heavenly or hellish experience here on earth. The choice is ours—always has been and always will! Free will—remember. We are the co-creators of our earthly experiences. God's perfect Universal laws are constantly at work to manifest our most prominent thoughts and desires. Our personal Karmic Quotient is the primary force affecting our daily lives.

Although our personal Karma is the primary force affecting us, it is not the only force. We are also subject to secondary Karmic influences such as clan Karma, national Karma and race Karma.

Clan Karma is the pain and suffering we endure as a consequence of our family members. When the law of balance causes pain and suffering to those we love, we can't help but experience pain as well. It seems terribly unfair when we suffer because of someone else, doesn't it? We feel like innocent bystanders or collateral damage. It's important to understand that all the suffering we endure as a direct result of the suffering inflicted upon our family members has a beneficial aspect. Their suffering is lowering their negative KQ and, at the same time, our suffering caused by them is also lowering our Karmic debts, bringing us that much closer to God. Suffering is not without purpose.

In any single lifetime, we may also bear the weight of our national Karma. When people form a new country and a new government, all the people of that nation share equally in the Karmic debts incurred on behalf of their government. We as citizens are responsible for the actions of our government. If we start a war, we are all responsible for the suffering incurred. If we are wounded in war or in a terrorist attack, we are helping to pay off the Karmic debts of our nation, helping the whole to achieve balance. Another secondary Karmic influence is that of the race of humanity as a whole. We are all responsible for the damage we are inflicting upon the planet. If we are made to suffer from a natural disaster like an earthquake or tornado, we are helping to balance out the debts of humanity.

Every cause must have an effect. We can't continue to pollute and cut down the rainforests without consequence. We are not separate from Nature! We are one with Nature. If we continue to pump huge amounts of carbon dioxide into the air, the polar ice caps are going to continue to melt. We will all suffer from global warming. Cause and effect. We cannot escape it. If we nurture Mother Earth, she will nurture us. If we abuse and harm Her, She will harm us. It's not complicated. We must choose wisely!

One last note on suffering. Our negative KQ is only reduced from suffering inflicted from without. If the law causes us misfortune, pain and suffering, or it comes from our family, loved ones, national or global issues, then our debts are reduced. However, self-inflicted pain and suffering has no benefit! If we manifest something that hurts us, it's our fault. If we choose to engage in anxiety, depression, drug abuse or illegal activities, there is NO benefit. Engaging in guilt and self-destructive behaviors is just wasteful and stupid! The Universal laws ensure that we will ultimately pay for our transgressions. Guilt is completely unnecessary and a waste of time and energy.

For example, my client John, who had all those auto accidents. The suffering incurred by the loss of his daughter reduced his negative KQ because it came from without. The suffering from the subsequent auto accidents did not reduce his KQ, because it was created by him through his thoughts manifested by the law of attraction and, therefore, had no beneficial value, Karmicly speaking. We are capable of manifesting anything we desire. If it's a selfish desire, we get the bill, in a manner of speaking. All selfish desires create negative Karma, and increase our debts. When we take something we have to pay for it. If we allow ourselves to receive something, there is no cost involved. If we use the law of attraction to manifest abundant wealth, we still have to pay for it. If we earn abundance through love and kindness and through good deeds, there is no cost involved. So it is possible to experience abundant wealth and prosperity without incurring any Karmic debt. Be careful what you ask for, because you just might get it! It's always our choice. We are all the architects of our future. I hope and pray we choose wisely. For us to reduce our Karmic debts, we first have to overcome the greatest of all obstacles on the Path to spiritual growth and evolution—our ego!

CHAPTER 9

EGO

What is ego? If I were to say, "That person has a big ego!," you would probably understand that to mean that they think a great deal about themselves. Narcissists, those in love with themselves, are usually accused of having a large ego. Even someone with excessive self-confidence would fit the description. However, this is not what I'm referring to here. Once we embark on the spiritual Path, we come across this term quite often within ancient texts and self-help books. My understanding of the ego has continued to change and evolve over the years, so I can only share with you my current understanding of it. I'm sure it will continue to evolve as I do.

Spiritually speaking, the ego is everything we think we are here on earth. It's every part of us that we feel is separate from God. It is synonymous with personality and character. Our egos, personalities, or characters are really a sum total of our beliefs and behavioral tendencies. It's the belief that we exist as an independent, separate individual. I, me and mine, are of the ego. They only exist while incarnate. They are not a part of our true Selves. There really is no us and them, there is only us. In reality there is no separateness, there is only oneness. In truth we are just points of light, equally perfect, unchanging, formless, eternal consciousness, Sons and

Daughters of Almighty God. If we believe we are anything other than this, it is an illusion and part of the ego. If I say, "I am my body," this is an illusion. If I say, "I am my thoughts," this is an illusion. If I say, "I am my desires, and my habits," these too are illusions. I say illusory, because in fact, the ego does not exist as a "real" thing. It is something we sustain with our incorrect thinking. It is illusory, because it can change or disappear altogether. In fact this is the essence of the spiritual Path, recognizing and transcending the illusory ego, and embracing and becoming our true Selves. Those who are enlightened are without an ego.

Eckhart Tolle is his book, *A New Earth*, defines ego as our "false self," the self created through our identification with form. We enhance our identity through our possessions, our families, our associations, our bodies and our thought forms and beliefs. He says, "When forms that you had identified with and that gave you your sense of self collapse or are taken away, it can lead to a collapse of the ego, since ego *is* identification with form. When there is nothing to identify with anymore, who are you?"

Provocative question, is it not?

WHAT IS THE EGO'S PURPOSE?

What is the purpose of the ego? I view the ego as a metering device. What is a metering device? It is something that controls flow. An example would be the holes in the top of a salt shaker. They allow a small amount of the total to flow out. The more holes there are, the more salt we get. A water dam is also a metering device. It holds back the majority of water, while allowing a small amount to pass through. The ego is metering out our spiritual evolution. The ego blocks the light of Truth, so only a small amount reaches us at any given time. The ego allows our evolution to unfold slowly, naturally over many lifetimes. Without egos, we would all instantly reach enlightenment.

So, once again we may be asking ourselves, if our evolution is unfolding naturally, why would we want to embark on an arduous spiritual path? The answer is still the same. Quality of Life! As long a we have to be here, shouldn't we want a life that is pleasant, fulfilling, meaningful and happy? Is your life full of peace, love and joy? Do you feel your life has meaning and purpose? If not, it certainly can be. We need only drop our illusions and embrace Truth.

Our ego is the only thing standing between us and God. If we can transcend our egos, we will come to know God. If we can transcend our egos, we will experience Heaven on earth. If we transcend our egos, we will experience no more suffering. Without an ego, we cannot suffer, for the ego is the source of our suffering. The ego is our biggest illusion and illusions are a source of suffering.

In the *Pistis Sophia*, Jesus refers to the ego as the "counterfeiting spirit."

> "...give the old soul a cup of forgetfulness, from the seed of wickedness, filled with all the various desires, and amnesia, and immediately, when the soul drinks from the cup, it forgets all the regions where it has been ...And that cup of water of forgetfulness takes on form outside the soul, and it imitates the soul in all its forms and resembles it, and this is what is called the *counterfeiting spirit*."

> "...and the *counterfeiting spirit* tempts the soul and continually forces it into all it's lawless actions, all it's

passions and all it's sin, and it holds steadfast to the soul and is antagonistic to it, forcing it to perform all this evil and all these sins. Now then Mary, this is in fact the enemy of the soul, and this coerces it into all sins."

" ...the *counterfeiting spirit* leads the soul to the Virgin of Light, the judge examines the soul and discovers that it has sinned and not finding within it the mysteries of the Light, she delivers it to one of her receivers, and her receiver takes it and sends it into the body, and it does not emerge from the transformation of the body until it has completed it's last circuit."

Some may be a little fearful about traversing the spiritual path to God. They may feel that to lose one's ego and become one with God is synonymous with annihilation or non-existence, similar to a raindrop falling into the ocean, becoming one with the ocean and losing its individuality. This also is an illusion, an untruth. We never lose our individuality, even when we are one with God. Oneness with God can be likened to a computer network. Our personal computer is a distinct individual unit, but when connected to the internet, it becomes one with all other computers connected to the internet. Unity Consciousness or oneness with God is similar to this. We maintain our individuality even when connected to the whole.

Once connected, we now have access to God's omni-present mind along with all others connected to God. For me, this is the essence of genius. A genius is not someone who knows everything, rather it is the ability to tap into the all-knowing mind of God existing within, to get the correct answer to any question posed. Genius is also knowing the right questions to ask. If you could tap into the omnipresent, omniscient mind of God and retrieve any truth desired, what would you ask? What do you desire to know?

Shortly after my spiritual awakening, while basking in the Light of the Lord, I had the strangest experience. At the time, I was completely ignorant of all things religious and spiritual. I had a million questions. As I sat in silence, contemplating the bizarre experience of actually conversing with Jesus, a man who supposedly died over two thousand years ago, I suddenly realized that every time I raised a question in my mind, I immediately received an answer to it. What was strange was that the answers seem to come from my own mind, as my own thought form. It was as if I was answering my own questions. But how could I? Why would I ask a question I already knew the answer to? The strange part was I really didn't know the answer until I asked the question. I didn't understand that I was communicating with the all-knowing, omnipresent mind of God, existing within myself. God's voice is so subtle, it's no louder than our own thoughts. I still have those experiences to this day; however, I can now recognize the difference between my thought forms and those of the Lord, although the difference is extremely subtle.

Another purpose of the ego is to help us develop compassion for others. It's only through our egos, our individuality, that we can imagine how any particular scenario might feel to us, thereby, knowing how others might be similarly affected. If something is painful to us, it is also probably painful to others. If something brings us joy, the same thing will most likely bring joy to others. The ego gives us a unique perspective. Through it we can imagine walking in someone else's shoes, in a manner of speaking. In this way, we can learn to develop compassion for others.

The ego is also the greatest motivating force in our lives. It spurs us into action by being our biggest cheerleader. The function of the ego is to bolster our confidence. It tells us constantly that we are better than everyone else. It tells us that our opinions are correct, and others are wrong. It tells us we are talented, attractive and likable. It assures us that we have a good handle on reality. What we think is true and correct and anyone who disagrees with us is just plain wrong.

We all have an ego and we all experience some level of fear. Fear is the balancing force of the ego. Too little fear and we rush headlong into dangerous situations. Too much fear and we become stifled, unable to act at all. We can see here just how important balance is in our lives.

The problem inherent with the ego is that it tries constantly to convince us of our superiority even when it's not true. When we believe everything the ego tells us, we can become delusional. This is quite apparent if you've ever watched the tryouts for American Idol. The worst singers imaginable truly believe in their hearts that they are better than everyone else. They have simply fallen prey to their own egos. After the judges have shed a little light of truth on them, one of two things happen. They either accept this new truth and have an emotional breakdown or their egos stand fast and they instead choose denial, which is the ego's defense mechanism. In their minds, they are right and the judges are wrong and no one can convince them otherwise. What's in their own minds has to be the truth, because their opinions have to be the correct ones.

A study of history should convince us that as a species, mankind as a whole is very slow to accept new truths. New ideas are always subject to doubt and scrutiny. Look how long it took for the majority to accept the truth that we are not the center of the universe, the earth is not flat and the sun does not revolve around us. Why are new ideas immediately rejected? The ego! The ego's job is to convince us that our current understanding is right, our perceptions are accurate and that we have a good handle on reality. When our personal truths are challenged, the ego goes into defense mode or denial. New ideas make us feel insecure, confused. Nobody likes the feeling of having the rug pulled out from underneath them. Our egos deal with this by choosing denial and continues to embrace old illusions because they feel less threatening. Changing our minds too quickly can be unsettling. A slow gradual change is more comforting to our fragile egos. Unfortunately, we live in a time of rapid, massive change. Truth is coming to us whether we are ready for it or not. It's imperative that we be more open-minded and go with the flow in regards to our rapid evolution in the coming years.

To survive in the new age, we must adapt and change right along with science, technology and changing global perspectives. Change is growth, growth is evolution, and evolution is always forward and positive. One of my favorite quotes is from Madame Blavatsky, the founder of modern Theosophy. She said, "We are all doomed to perfection." See the Light of a New Age dawning. Embrace the Light. Embrace the Truth. Once the Truth takes hold within us, the world becomes a much less scary place. Embrace Truth and we will know Peace and Happiness. If we continue to hold on to old illusions, we are sure to experience more suffering. Wake up Brothers and Sisters, wake up! See the illusory ego for what it is, and come to know your true Selves.

HOW DO WE RECOGNIZE THE EGO?

How do we recognize our egos? First and foremost, the ego can be heard as a voice in our head. Everyone has an internal dialogue, whether they are conscious of it or not. Don't you generally think about what you are going to say before you say it? Don't we rehearse potential conversations within our minds? We all talk to ourselves—it's perfectly normal. The problem arises when we identify with the voices in our minds as being us. If we believe that every thought we experience is born of our own mind, then we can be easily manipulated by our ego. Truth is, everyone hears at least two distinct voices in their minds, and these two voices are always giving us contradictory messages. That's why we are so confused. That's why we really don't know what we want. This internal conflict is the primary source for all external conflicts.

What is within us is reflected outside of us. This is commonly know as projection. We are constantly projecting our internal issues onto other people around us. Whatever our beliefs, they are projected into the world out there. We don't see the world as it really is, instead we see it as we believe it is. Our perception of reality is but a reflection of our inner reality, our beliefs, our philosophy, our own personal paradigms.

Most people are aware of only one voice within their own minds. The loudest, most insistent and dominant voice we hear is that of our egos. The second is far more subtle. It's the still small voice of our true Selves, our Spirit Selves. This is the voice of our conscience, trying to keep us from doing things we know to be wrong. It's also the voice of intuition, and the source of inspiration. Carlos Castaneda's teacher, don Juan Matus, referred to the ego as a *"foreign installation."*

In *The Active Side of Infinity*, he says, "…I repeat to you what I said before about our two minds. One is our true mind, the product of all our life experiences, the one that rarely speaks, because it has been defeated and relegated to obscurity. The other, the mind we use daily for everything we do, is a *foreign installation*." Every one of us human beings has two minds. One is totally ours and it is like a faint voice that always brings us order, directness, purpose. The other mind is a *foreign installation*. It brings us conflict, self-assertion, doubts, hopelessness."

This dichotomy is best represented by the archetypal devil whispering in one ear and an angel whispering in the other. We all experience this internal conflict. One voice would have us succumb to every selfish impulse, while the other is suggesting we think of others first. One is tempting us to be bad, while the other is urging us to be good. But we can serve only one master, so we must choose which to follow. The unenlightened masses follow the selfish impulse of their egos, while those traversing the spiritual path suppress selfish desires and seek to improve themselves by following the suggestions of the still small voice of God within.

It's imperative that we understand the workings of our minds. The human brain can be likened to a CB radio. It can both send and receive messages. Every message received is not necessarily self-generated. We can pick up thought forms from other people, from the universe at large, or from God. Illusionists who read minds are not really reading minds, but rather broadcasting messages that are then picked up by the mind of their subject. They are adept at planting thoughts in the minds of others, who readily accept them as their own. Without this understanding, we are open to the influence of others and our selfish, angry egos.

Another way to recognize the ego within is to observe our thoughts, feelings and re-actions whenever we feel offended or angered. Only egos are offended. Our egos are responsible for our sense of self-importance. The more respect we demand from others, the greater the ego's influence over us. If we are constantly being offended by the actions of others, then we have a very active ego indeed. If we are constantly judging others, criticizing others, or gossiping about others, that is the ego at work. To recognize the ego is to bring awareness to our thoughts, our words, our habits, our reactions, our intentions and our motivations. If we scrutinize every thought and impulse, we will surely perceive our own ego.

How Do We Overcome the Ego?

Once we see it in action, then what? How do we transcend our ego? The first step is simply awareness. We have to recognize a problem before we go about fixing it. If we decide for ourselves that we wish to grow spiritually, the first step is to become more aware of the still small voice of God within us. This may take some time and practice. I have found stillness meditation to be an effective method for this. I simply sit quietly and witness all the thought forms streaming through my mind. Selfish, self-centered thoughts are of my ego. I simply ignore them and listen carefully for their counterpart. These opposing thoughts, those that are selfless in nature are most likely from my spiritual Self, my true Self. For best results, I suggest asking God for His Wisdom and Guidance. Ask a specific question (prayer), and listen intently for the answer(meditation). In time, you will be able to perceive the difference between

your ego and your Spirit Self. Only then can you successfully traverse the spiritual path in life.

The second step is in making a conscious choice to ignore
selfish impulses and instead, follow the urgings of our soul,
our True Selves. This is much easier said than done. It requires
persistent sincere effort. After all, we have been conditioned
our whole lives to listen to and follow the urgings of our
egos. It will take some time to reverse this habit. And it is just
that—a habit. But all habits can be overcome in time. This
too is essentially the nature of spiritual growth and development. Becoming aware of our unconscious behaviors and
then consciously seeking to change them. Some will insist
that people don't change. And it's true that we don't change
accidentally. Change is brought about through the intention
of change. We have to want to change and we have to work
hard at it, but it can be done. I have changed so much in
the last fifteen years, it's mind-boggling. I'm a completely
different person. To begin the process, however, we must
first change our beliefs. Action follows thought. If we change
our beliefs, our actions are sure to follow. For me, the first
belief that changed was my belief in God. Once I experienced
His presence and then accepted this experience as a reality,
the process of change unfolded rapidly. Once I believed that
there were two distinct and different voices in my mind, I
was then capable of choosing between them. Only after I
recognized my ego, could I go about trying to overcome it.
Conscious evolution had begun. Enlightenment is a choice
we must make for ourselves. First, we must become aware
that we have a choice and secondly, we must actively make
a choice. We all have the gift of free will. We can continue
to serve ourselves, our selfish egos, or we can serve God
and our fellow man. One path is wide and many follow it. It

leads to endless incarnations, pain and suffering. The other is narrow and few find it. But those that choose to walk the narrow path find enlightenment, peace, love, and happiness, and ultimately heaven. The choice is ours.

CHAPTER 10

NOW

Time Versus the Present Moment

God is. God is here. God is here now. Is the "now" really necessary? Isn't it redundant? Think about it. We can't have one without the other. If we're here, it's now. If it's now, we're here. We can't be somewhere else now—right? If it's now we are here. Einstein figured out that time and space are not separate, so he called it *space-time*. Space-time is like a fabric that twists and bends in the presence of stars and planets. He postulated this in his papers on the Theory of Relativity in 1907. His theories were proven fact in 1922 when during a complete solar eclipse, the stars around the sun were photographed. The photos proved that the light from distant stars was distorted around the sun exactly as Einstein predicted. Simply put, wherever we are in space and time is also when we are. As we peer into deep space, we are also looking into the past. Einstein also discovered that matter is energy—$E = mc^2$. He proved that matter is really just compressed light. He won the Nobel prize in 1923 for his work on the photo-electric effect. In this repeatable experiment, he proved that light has the properties of both a wave and a particle. When the electron microscope was invented, we learned that when matter is looked at very closely, nothing is really there. Particles are made up of 99.99% empty space! This is why I choose to view this world as being less solid and real, and more like an artificial simulation, like a 3-D fully interactive hologram. For me, the only thing that is truly real is God and His Kingdom.

Do you remember Sept.11, 2001? I think any adult alive at that time remembers that day very well. It was a monumental event in our country's history. So monumental in fact that a live image of the burning twin towers was broadcast across the entire globe. Think about this. The entire world watched at the same moment as the twin towers collapsed. Those on the East coast experienced the horror at approximately 10 A.M. However, those in California watched it unfold at 7 A.M.. Those in Europe watched the tragedy unfold at 3 in the afternoon. But get this, those watching from New Zealand watched the towers fall in the early morning hours of the next day. That's right, they experienced 9/11 on 9/12! Where you are is also when you are. If I were in New York at 10 A.M. watching the first tower fall, and was then magically transported to New Zealand in time to watch the second tower fall, I would have effectively travelled forward in time, to the next day. However, all experience is perceived in the present moment regardless of what the calendar or wristwatch says. This is the *now* we need to know about. Everyone, regardless of where they were, watched the towers fall at the same moment, just not at the same *time*. That moment is the ever present moment, the now moment. The present moment, the now, is ever unfolding eternally.

Since the birth of the universe, there has existed the

present moment, whether or not there were people around to observe it. Think about this. Birds don't need to check a calendar to know when to fly south. Bears don't need to check a calendar to know when to hibernate. Flowers don't need to check a calendar to know when to bloom. Nature functions perfectly without timepieces. In reality there is no time, only eternal duration. The present moment is real, eternal and unchanging. What happens in the present moment seems to constantly change, however, the moment itself is ever-present and unchanging. It is real. It's the only space-time in which we can experience God.

It's impossible to experience anything in the future. The future is an illusion, part of the manmade construct of time. I realized this once while in a bar that had a sign posted, "Free beer tomorrow!" That illusory construct includes the idea of a past and a future. We cannot experience the past. We can only experience a reproduction of the past, which we experience in the present moment. It's the same with the future. We can construct a fantasy future in our minds, but we are still experiencing it in the present moment. All experience is in the present moment. Whether we are reminiscing about the past, or fantasizing about the future, or paying attention to something happening in front of us, all experience is in the present moment, or the now. God can only be experienced in the present moment, here and now. Life can only be lived in the present moment, here and now. Enlightenment can only be experienced in the present moment, here and now.

Why is it important that we make the distinction between the current time and the present moment? If we're not planning on traversing the spiritual path in this life, then the difference is unimportant. However if we wish to make progress, this understanding is paramount. If we choose to seek God, His wisdom and guidance, we must live in the present moment, for that is the only space-time in which He can be found. The present moment is the abode of God. Time is the abode of the ego. Unfortunately, the ego knows all too well that God resides in the present moment and will do all it can to keep us from going there. The ego knows that its survival depends on keeping us from God, keeping us out of the present moment. We can only serve one master, and we are always choosing between the ego and God. The ego is fighting for our attention, while God is sitting back patiently waiting for us to choose Him. It's completely up to us, free will.

You might be thinking that if you are awake, you are in the present moment, right? With a cursory glance this might appear to be the case, but upon closer examination we will discover that in fact we spend an extremely small amount of our waking hours, completely awake and aware of the present moment. Most of the time, our minds are only partially aware of what's going on around us. We are usually engaged in fantasy or reminiscing, wandering back and forth between past and future, avoiding the present moment whenever possible.

Let me give you an example. Do you remember the first time you drove a car? Most people do. Why? When we do something for the very first time, we have to engage more of our awareness, put our full attention to the task at hand. Focused awareness is what creates indelible memories. The first time we drove a car, it was exciting with a hint of danger. Driving is a important right of passage for most people. When we first put that car in gear, we engaged our full attention, and an indelible memory remains. I'm sure most have also had the experience of driving home from work, getting home and realizing you have no memory of the drive home. Does this sound familiar? It should be. It's the nature of our minds. Once we become familiar with something, say driving, it no longer requires our full attention. After a while we learn to drive at an unconscious level, while our minds are engaged in other things. We can recall what we were thinking about, but not the drive home. Auto accidents are caused by our egos, distracting us from the present moment.

Once we label something or pass judgment on a person or situation, we stop paying attention to it. One cursory glance and our mind goes, I know what that is, move on to the next thing. When we were very young, experiencing many firsts, we paid special attention to everything. As we get older, we judge rather than look. Life becomes boring, predictable and unexciting. We think we see what's going on, however, we are instead just taking an inventory of our preconceived judgments. We must learn to once again see the world with fresh eyes, taking nothing for granted. Life viewed without judgments is then once again mysterious, exciting and beautiful.

Developing present moment awareness is indispensible for those desiring spiritual growth, and a closer personal relationship with God. We can communicate with God only in the present moment. We can hear His guidance only in a stilled, quiet, present moment. Seek God here and now, and you will surely find Him. Ask for His guidance and you will surely receive it. Thirst for His righteousness and you will be filled with His Wisdom

How to Develop Present Moment Awareness

How do we go about cultivating present moment awareness? How do we seek and find, ask and receive? How do we become filled with His righteousness and wisdom? The answer is quite simple, but unfortunately, not easy. What is required of us is willpower, dedication and focus. We have to practice mental stillness. We have to use our willpower to turn off our internal dialogue. We have to stop talking to ourselves. Have you ever tried to focus on just one thing for any length of time? It's extremely challenging! At first be happy with just a few seconds. It requires sincere effort and dedication to every single day set aside some time to practice stilling our minds. Much practice is required to extend those few seconds into a few minutes. Trust me, this practice is well worth the effort. Once the internal dialogue is suppressed, then we can focus on listening to the still small voice of God within. We need only to speak to Him clearly and precisely. We can seek His wisdom and guidance or we can ask Him to reveal Himself to us. We then keep our minds still and quiet and listen intently for His voice welling up from within us. Or we can pay close attention to what's happening within our bodies. His presence is felt as the rising emotions of peace, love and joy. If we feel happy for no reason, it means God is expressing His love for us.

It sounds simple enough—then why is it so difficult? The ego is fighting us every step of the way. How? Distraction! Every time we attempt present moment awareness, the ego distracts us with either a memory or a fantasy. The ego is insidious in this respect. It will pull out every trick in the book to keep you out of the present moment. Why? Because it losses power over us when we connect with God. The ego is then facing annihilation or death. Once God is perceived as real and the ego illusory, it fades away into nonexistence. Our real Self, our Spirit Self is now in control of our lives. The whole world and everything and everyone in it become more interesting, more mysterious, more beautiful. We are now ready to fulfill our true purpose, our true mission here on earth. We can now pay off our Karmic debts, learn our life lessons and ultimately return home to our Heavenly Father.

There are a few things we can do to that are very effective at developing present moment awareness. First, we find something in the present moment to focus on. If we focus on something happening here and now, we are then in the present moment. Our breathing is happening always. No matter where we are, we can stop and focus on our breath. Breath awareness is an ancient and effective method for bringing us into the now. We simply empty our minds as much as possible, turn off our internal dialogue and focus intently on every in breath and out breath. At first, counting to ten on each breath works well at keeping us focused. The ancients believed that the mind and the breath are intimately linked. The more we breathe, the more thoughts enter the mind. The less we breathe, the fewer thoughts we have. They sought the breathless state with no thoughts. This is possible with much practice.

The next thing we can do is to eliminate habits. Habitual behavior is unconscious behavior. Unconsciousness is the opposite of enlightenment. The unenlightened live their lives in relative unconsciousness. They are only partially aware of what's happening around them. The enlightened are fully aware at all times, fully awake in the present moment. Developed habits require very little focused attention.

It's very easy to engage in fantasy and reminiscing while engaged in habitual behaviors. Driving is a great example. After years of practice, we learn to multitask while driving. Personally I have witnessed people doing things like talking on the phone, texting, reading, applying makeup, eating, and drinking while driving. I find this disturbing and obviously very dangerous. Multitasking is the opposite of focused attention. It's like white light being diffracted into a rainbow. Focused thought is more like a laser beam. We must avoid multitasking whenever possible. We must focus our awareness like a laser in order to hear the voice of God within.

How to Reduce Anxiety

What is anxiety? Anxiety is fear experienced in the body as a direct result of fearful thoughts in the mind. All emotions felt within the body are linked directly to thoughts in the mind. If we reminisce about a pleasant memory in the past, we experience peace and joy in the body. If we fantasize about a fearful future, we experience fear in the body. If we fantasize about sex, we experience arousal in the body. There is a direct link between mind and body, thought and emotion. Anxiety is a result of our egos distracting us out of a peaceful, pleasant, present moment. We are instead thinking about a fearful future. Instead of experiencing peace in a peaceful present moment, we experience anxiety instead. Anxiety is useless, unpleasant, destructive, and entirely unnecessary. Anxiety can be overcome by the practice of present moment awareness. If we are always in the present moment we will experience much less fear and anxiety.

Anxiety is also produced in the body whenever we engage in thoughts that include phrases, such as *would have, could have* and *should have.* These are all fantasy projections of the mind. They do not exist. These thoughts produce guilt and regret. They are useless and destructive to our health and well-being. These thoughts are an affront to what is. We cannot change what is. Our only healthy choice is to accept what is and deal with that. Fighting what is, is like swimming up stream against a current. We waste a lot of time and energy and we get absolutely nowhere. One of my favorite expressions is, "It is what it is." Getting upset or angry won't change the facts. Banging our head against the wall will only give us a headache. Engaging in thoughts that begin with, "If only" or "it might have" will not change the current situation. They only serve to add guilt, resentment, regret, fear and anxiety into our lives. We need only to recognize these thought patterns and choose to embrace the truth instead. The truth of what is. Accepting the current situation and dealing with what is, is far more effective at reducing and overcoming excessive anxiety. To experience a life filled with unending peace, love and happiness, we need to be awake and aware in the present moment always, and being accepting of what is, right here and right now. How do we become aware and awake always, and stay in the present moment? How do we recognize our habitual behaviors, the ones that steal our peace and cause pain and suffering? We have to tap into our real Selves, the Observer within.

I have to thank author, Eckhart Tolle, for helping me to understand *The Power of Now.* I dedicate this entire chapter to him. He has contributed more than any other contemporary writer to my understanding of present moment awareness and the ego. I highly recommend his books.

CHAPTER 11

OBSERVER

THE AMERICAN AGENDA FOR SUCCESS

Every philosopher throughout history has asked themselves the same fundamental questions, such as, "Who am I? Where did I come from? What am I supposed to be doing here? Where do we go from here? Does God really exist? What is the meaning of Life?" For the first thirty-six years of my life, I was an agnostic. I believed in the possibility of a God, however, I had never witnessed proof of His existence. My family and friends were not religious and never talked about God. I didn't care at all about philosophy, religion or spirituality. I was a pragmatist, a realist, a materialistic entrepreneur. My main goal in life was to become a self-made millionaire like my father before me. I felt confident that this was my destiny. My desires centered around sex and money, and in that order. All my energy went into getting laid and getting paid. I had bought into the American agenda.

What is the American agenda? It's the unwritten, unspoken formula for success and happiness. See if this sounds familiar. As children, we are encouraged to obey all adults without question. We are to be seen and not heard. We are to keep out of trouble, do well in school, and we are supposed to be like others, fit in, follow the crowd, color inside the lines. Independent thinking is discouraged. As we get older, we are expected to find a good job, settle down with a mate, buy a home and raise a family. We are supposed to work really hard for forty or fifty years and then retire. Happiness is to be experienced in retirement as we spend our life savings having fun. Does this sound about right to you? If we are following this agenda, we are engaged in the "rat race."

If it was a race, I felt I was definitely in the lead. I kept my nose clean as a kid and I did well in school. I got into a good university and I married my high school sweetheart, the love of my life. We had three beautiful children. I was part-owner of a successful family business, making lots of money working in management. I had a company car, an expense account, plenty of notoriety and respect. For all intents and purposes, I was a success. I had a bright future indeed. However, there was one big problem. With all my apparent success, I should of been happy, but instead I was depressed, exceedingly unhappy. The worst part was, I didn't know why. I had everything going for me. I was following the American agenda to the tee. There was no reason I should not have been happy, but I just wasn't. I still felt incomplete, unful-filled. There was a nagging emptiness within me that I just couldn't fill. I became more and more self-indulgent trying to attain some level of happiness. I tried compensating by overindulging in food. Instead of becoming happier I just got fatter, and more unhappy. Nothing I tried would bring me any real happiness or a sense of completeness or wholeness.

As my frustration mounted I felt I needed to make major changes in my life. I became disenchanted with the family business, so I quit. I ventured out into the world to make my own fortune as a wallpaper installer. I was very skilled and had plenty of contacts for work. My ego had me convinced that I was as capable as my dad in finding success. I was wrong. I was not my father. I was convinced that his talents were my talents. His success was my success. Anything he could do, I could do. However, once I was on my own away from his business, his support and influence, I realized that my opinions about myself were over-inflated and just plain wrong. Truth started to seep into my awareness. My faults and weaknesses became increasingly apparent. The combination of depression and financial stress proved too much for me to bear, and on Christmas Eve 1996, I experienced a full-blown meltdown, an emotional catharsis unparalleled in my life so far. From my perspective, life as I knew it was over. In my own mind, I was a complete failure. I was so angry at myself. I hated myself. I just knew there was no one else to blame but myself. I could see clearly that my problems all stemmed from a series of really bad choices—*my* choices. I could see that the suffering I was experiencing was due to cause and effect. My choices were the cause, my suffering was the effect. And although this was now apparent, the way through this crisis was not. I had no idea what I was supposed to do next. All I could think of was intense self-loathing. I rejected myself. I didn't want to be me anymore. I cursed myself repeatedly.

In my desperation, I decided to reach out to God. I knew I needed help, and I also knew I had no idea how to help myself. I beseeched Him to make Himself known to my heart and to my mind. I needed to know that He existed. My life depended on it. I could sense my approaching death. I had no desire to go on living the way things were. I just couldn't take it anymore. I prayed and prayed and prayed with all the sincerity and emotion I could muster. I asked

God to reveal the truth to me. "Who am I, really? How did I get here? Why am I here? What am I supposed to be doing here? Where do I go from here? Can you hear me? Can you help me? How do I find true and lasting happiness? I was so exhausted I drifted off to sleep in my spa. I had a dream of Jesus. I awoke a couple hours later and finally went off to bed. In the morning, I awoke feeling really good. I was happy and carefree. All my problems felt as if they were a million miles away. Over the course of the next few weeks, I experienced an ever-increasing sense of well-being. I experienced emotions I had never before experienced—emotions like Love, Peace, Happiness, Forgiveness, Hope and Faith. They were wonderful, however, also a little disconcerting because of their intensity—especially my ever-increasing feelings of love for God and Jesus. How could I experience love for someone I didn't believe in? I always thought forgiveness was a verb, something we did. I was experiencing it as an emotion. I felt forgiven. I felt reborn. I felt like I was starting life over. But how could I feel forgiven when nobody had forgiven me of anything? Why was I so happy? There was no apparent reason for it. It didn't make sense to me. I was exceedingly happy and yet very confused. No matter what the nature of thoughts within my mind, I experienced within my body an unshakable Peace. It was beautiful and troubling all at the same time. What is going on? Why does life feel so different? Did I really connect with God? Did He really hear me and respond to my prayers? This was the only answer that made any sense. What do I do now? Who can I talk to about this? I didn't know anyone who knew God. I decided to pray once again to God for some understanding. When I did, I experienced a flashback of sorts—a memory or a dream from Christmas Eve emerged from my subconscious. I clearly remembered having a short conversation with Jesus. Could it be possible it wasn't a dream? Does Jesus still live? Is Jesus God? Did God send Jesus? Or did God reveal Himself in a form I could understand? Did God really reveal Himself to me? Why me?? It just doesn't make sense. Millions of people pray every day for their whole lives and as far as I know, they don't experience God. God doesn't speak directly to people, does He? People who claim to hear the voice of God are considered to be insane. Nobody is going to believe that I found God after praying just once. Why would He reveal Himself to me? Who am I??

WHO ARE WE, REALLY?

A philosopher was born. I was plagued with a million questions. I needed to find some answers. I now had within me a burning desire, an unquenchable passion for discovering the Truth. Who or what is God and who am I? I started reading every spiritual text I could get my hands on. I kept my revelations to myself, because I knew there was still the possibility that I had lost my mind. Life was now a completely different experience, I was living an entirely new reality. I knew that either I was insane, or God had revealed Himself to me. I was desperately hoping it was the latter. However, if this was insanity, it wasn't so bad. I was at the very least happy for a change. Very, very happy—dare I say it, insanely happy?

It took many years before I could openly discuss my spiritual experiences. Eventually I became convinced that I was indeed sane and God really did exist. He convinced me of His existence. My Faith in Him has grown to the point that I am now willing to put myself out on a limb by putting my beliefs and experiences in writing. If I can help but one person to find God and His Peace and Happiness, then it is worth the potential ridicule.

How do you feel about yourself? Do you love yourself? Do you hate yourself? Have you ever given it much thought? How can you love or hate yourself? Who is doing the loving and who is being loved? Who is doing the hating and who is being hated? Think about it. We are of a dual nature. We are two-fold. Who is "I" and who is my "self"?

As we discussed earlier, the self is our ego, our personality, our lower nature. If we can have an opinion about our own personality, who is doing the judging? The "I" that is judging our personality is our true Self, our higher nature or the Observer. The Observer is our Soul, our Spirit Self. It is the formless, eternal consciousness inhabiting the body. We are not a body with a Soul, but a Soul with a body. The body is the temporary vehicle of the Observer. The Observer is the recorder of all thoughts, words and deeds within each lifetime. When the Observer leaves the body, it takes with it all memories, lessons learned and love connections made. While in between incarnations, the Observer exists as pure consciousness, equally perfect with all other Souls, one with each other, one with God and one with the entire Universe. Our personalities, our bodies, our wealth and possessions, our power and influence are all left behind.

The Observer is Real. It is eternal, perfect and unchanging. It is the us that reincarnates into new and different bodies. The vehicle is unimportant. Whether it is beautiful or ugly, healthy or unhealthy, black or white is unimportant. The body and the personality are just vehicles for our earthly Karma. The Observer's purpose is to assist in the evolution of the ego, our lower nature and the working out of our Karmic debts. Once the Observer gains control over the body, then and only then can real progress be made. An enlightened person is one whose Soul is in charge, one whose illusory ego has been transcended.

SELF-OBSERVATION

So how do we use this understanding of the Observer to grow spiritually? Most people use the majority of their conscious awareness to perceive the world outside of them. We are obsessed with what other people are doing and saying. We sit in front of the television watching an endless loop of world news. We think it's our responsibility to know everything that's happening all over the world. We read tabloids and magazines, so we can keep up with what famous people are doing. We spy on our neighbors. We're obsessed with social networks like Twitter and Facebook, so we know what's happening with our family and friends. Why? The same reason we don't spend much time in the present moment. Our egos! The ego knows that God exists in the present moment, so it distracts us with fantasy and reminiscing. And it also knows that God exists within ourselves, so it distracts us by keeping our focus on the world, out there. For its own survival it distracts us from the present moment and from what's happening within. If we look within we may find God, so the ego urges us to stay focused instead on what's happening outside of us.

Judgment of others comes from the ego. Gossiping about others is of the ego. The desire to change others comes from the ego. The desire to change the world comes from the ego. To grow spiritually, we have to suppress those urgings from the ego and instead, use our inherent awareness to perceive what's happening within. God can be found here and now, in the present moment right within our very selves. But before we can go there, we need to recognize and suppress our egos. We simply change our focus—forget about what's happening in the world out there. Forget about what other people are doing and saying and instead, turn our perception inward.

We must examine our own beliefs, our motivations and intentions. Most importantly we need to examine our own behaviors and habits. Specifically our unconscious re-actions to the world out there. For example, we can observe ourselves when we get angry. As I said before, only egos get angry, so we are essentially watching our egos.

Anger is a universal emotion to which we can all relate. Anger is a destructive emotion, detrimental to our spiritual growth and evolution. Anger can easily lead to violence, pain and suffering. Violence is a negative Karma-producing behavior. It can even cost us our freedom. Our freedom of choice. And we need to be able to choose to grow and evolve. When we are overcome with anger, it is as if we become possessed by it. We lose control over ourselves. We are essentially acting out unconsciously. Unconscious behavior is the opposite of enlightened behavior. So how do we avoid this dangerous and destructive emotion? We simply use the Observer within us to bring awareness to our unconsciousness. Awareness negates unconsciousness.

At first, we may not become aware until the anger has subsided. We recognize after the fact that we became angry. It's important that we replay the tapes within our minds. We go back and witness the process. We see the rising emotion, how we felt and what we did. With continued practice, we can become aware of our unconsciousness while in the midst of being angry. We recognize that we are angry right now. When this happens, something amazing happens. Bringing awareness into an unconscious action is like shining a light into a darkened room full of scary shadows. The light of Truth makes the shadows, the illusions, and the anger disappear. Becoming aware of anger in the present moment can make it vanish. This is the process of developing self-control, the essence of spiritual growth and development.

Eventually, with more practice, we become aware and conscious of anger welling up within us. We recognize that we are getting angry right now. This can easily stop the process in its tracks, keeping us from becoming angry altogether. An enlightened individual can never become offended or angry by the actions of another. They have perfect self-control. With this understanding we can see how God too is beyond anger or wrath.

The process of enlightenment is synonymous with the process of eliminating all unconscious, Karma-producing behaviors. To be enlightened is to be always fully awake in the present moment, and aware of all our thoughts, emotions and behavioral tendencies. To be enlightened is know that we are not our personalities, our bodies or our desires. To be enlightened is to know that we are really the Observer within.

CHAPTER 12

WORK

Everything presented up to this point is merely philosophy, a belief system, a personal paradigm. Embracing Truth is the first step upon the Path of Enlightenment or the Path of Righteousness, if you prefer. Once we change our minds about the nature of Reality, progress begins. Engaging in spiritual studies and philosophy is an important first step, however, it is just talking the talk. Acquiring wisdom is essential to our growth and evolution, but meaningless, if it is not applied in our lives. I define wisdom as the proper application of knowledge. For example, man has discovered the knowledge necessary for splitting the atom. That knowledge can be applied to either the creation of cheap energy used for the benefit of mankind or it can be applied to the creation of atomic weapons used for the destruction of mankind. Which do you think is the right use of this knowledge? The former—right? Applied wisdom is righteousness or right-use-ness.

Once we acquire wisdom, it must be applied to have power. At some point we have to walk the walk, as it were. We have to practice what we preach. We have to live our truth rather than just give it lip service. Only then do we make genuine progress on the Path to God.

In the New Testament, Jesus said in Matthew 7:5, "You hypocrite, first take the plank out of your own eye, and then you will see clearly to remove the speck from your brother's eye." This is why I suggested in the previous chapter that we stop paying attention to the world out there and to what other people are doing and saying, but instead focus on what's happening within us. Before we can attempt to correct others, we first have to recognize and correct our own faults. We first need to "Be perfect as your Heavenly Father is perfect." (Matthew 5:48)

Only after we have perfected ourselves can we be of service to others. Otherwise we are only projecting our illusions and untruths onto them, and this benefits no one. We are then like "The blind leading the blind, likely to fall into a pit." (Matthew 15:14) The acquisition and application of real wisdom can take many years or many lifetimes. It is, however, a process that we will all undertake at some point in our evolution. It is a requisite of ascension. We can not proceed to the next level until we have mastered this one.

How do we achieve perfection? How do we master this level? How do we *remove the plank from our own eyes*? We must tap into our real selves, our spiritual or God selves, the Observer within us. It's all about awareness and observation. No corrections can be made until that which needs correction is recognized and identified. We can't fix a problem we don't see. Once we tap into the awareness of the Observer within, we can become cognizant of our habits, our unconscious reactions and behaviors. Once we see our angry egos, we can then take steps to overcome it. Self-observation and then self-correction are the essence of the spiritual path to God. Self-realization is synonymous with God realization, which is synonymous with enlightenment.

It is at this stage that the men are separated from the boys, so to speak. It takes a lot of heart, sincerity and fortitude to withstand the impact of Truth, as it relates to our very selves. Few have the courage to stare headlong into the mirror for any length of time while observing their own faults, weaknesses and illusions. Why? Because it is a gut-wrenching and nauseating experience.

I remember being depressed, ashamed and embarrassed. I didn't participate in any spiritual study groups for a time, because I felt transparent. I thought everyone could see my faults as I did. It was one of the worst periods of my life. Eventually, the fog lifted and I began to feel some optimism again. I then dedicated myself to self-improvement. I wanted to be a better man. I wanted and needed to have self-respect. It was at this point that I stopped paying attention to the world out there, and started focusing on what was happening within myself. As soon as I recognized something about myself that I felt needed improvement, I set about the task of change. Herein is the real work.

I call it *work*, because I soon realized that change is difficult. Our habits are deeply engrained within us. We can't just wish them away. Habitual behaviors are literally hardwired into our brains. To eradicate a bad habit, a negative Karma-producing habit, like getting angry, we have to replace it with a new more appropriate behavior. It requires us to recognize an unconscious act in the midst of it, and then stop it by doing something else instead. Only in this way can we rewire the brain. We have to stop the synapses while they are firing to create a new behavior. This takes practice, practice and more practice. It's hard work, but well worth the effort.

Eradicating illusions requires us to embrace the Truth. Eradicating bad habits requires us to embrace good habits. Eradicating drama, misfortune and suffering requires us to embrace the Universal laws of God. Eradicating the ego requires us to embrace selfless service to others. If we are in the conscious pursuit of becoming a better person then we engaged in our own spiritual evolution. If our lives revolve around the pursuit of wealth, power, influence, fame, security and pleasure, then we are wasting our time chasing after illusions. They will all be left behind when our Soul departs the body.

We do, however, get to take with us our memories, so create as many pleasant ones as you can. We do get to take with us our spiritual progress, our lessons learned. Our hard work will definitely benefit us in our next incarnation. We also get to take with us our love connections. True love is real, enduring and eternal. Love transcends time and space. Our loving Father makes sure we reincarnate again and again with those we love and those that love us. Love is the only worthwhile pursuit in life. Forget about wealth and fame— seek only Love. Seek and you shall find. Give Love and you will surely receive it. This is God's promise to us. We are here to learn how to give abundantly from the heart. We are here to learn how to love unconditionally. We are here to learn how to forgive everyone and everything. We are here to learn how to be perfect as our Heavenly Father is perfect. We are His children after all.

VIRTUE VS. VICE

So how do we go about becoming perfect? First thing we must do is to perform an honest self-evaluation. It's imperative that we become acquainted with our own strengths and weaknesses. After we become conscious of our weaknesses, then the real work begins. It takes a lot of hard work to change our weaknesses into strengths, our vices into virtues. Seven vices are paired up with seven virtues in the following list:

VIRTUES AND VICES

Humility vs. Pride

Patience vs. Wrath

Kindness vs. Envy

Diligence vs. Sloth

Charity vs. Greed

Temperance vs. Gluttony

Chastity vs. Lust

HUMILITY VS. PRIDE

Answer these questions as honestly as you can:

Do you consider yourself to be proud or humble? Are you proud as a peacock or as humble as a Buddhist monk? Perhaps somewhere in between? Don't know?

Are you almost always sure that your opinions are the correct ones? Are you quick to tell others that they are wrong? Do you demand respect from others? Are you rude to those who you feel are beneath you? Do you refuse to do anything in public that might make you appear silly or weak? Do you refuse to bow down or submit to those in authority? Do you lash out at those who don't treat you with respect? Do you argue with or attack those who tell you that you are wrong?

Are you convinced that you are more talented than those in your field? Do you get upset with those who don't give you compliments when they should? Do you refuse to admit being wrong even when you know you are? Do you intentionally hang out with people who are less attractive than you?

Do you refuse to work in a job where you have to serve others? Do you find it difficult to apologize or admit that you're wrong, or ask for forgiveness? Do you get frustrated when others fail to recognize your true talents?

If you answered **YES** to any of these questions, then you should work at becoming more humble. Pride is of the ego. Refer back to Chapter 9 on ego. To grow spiritually, we must overcome our egos. Those who approach God with humility or their soul are exalted, while those that approach God with pride or the ego are humbled. In the New Testament, Jesus gave us a great example of humility. Even though He was the Master, He washed the feet of His disciples. Even though He had greater power, more authority and greater wisdom, He was humble to those around Him. In John 13:14, Jesus said, "Now that I your Lord and Teacher, have washed your feet, you also should wash one another's feet." He did not demand worship and praise from His followers. He was also not afraid to be seen associating with tax collectors and sinners.

To be truly humble is to believe that you are no better than anyone else. For all men are created equal. That is truth. To embrace humility is to embrace this Truth. To practice humility is to constantly treat others as equals, regardless of their appearance, social stature, wealth or notoriety.

PATIENCE VS. WRATH

Answer these questions as honestly as you can:

- When you are standing in line at a retail outlet or grocery store, and there are at least three people in front of you, do you wait quietly until it's your turn? Do you jump from line to line hoping to find a faster one? Do you complain to the manager and insist they open another register? Do you leave your purchases at the checkout and storm out of the store, vowing never to return?

- When someone cuts you off and then drives too slowly in front of you, do you wait patiently until they move over? Do you curse at them loudly and flip them the bird? Do you tailgate them closely, while blinking your headlights and honking your horn? Do you encourage them to pull off the road, so you can pummel them into a bloody pulp?

- When your children fail to follow your directions, do you calmly repeat yourself as often as needed until they comply? Do you curse and scream at them until they comply? Do you threaten bodily harm unless they comply? Do you beat them senseless for not complying?

If you answered **YES** to anything other than the very first question, you should work on becoming more patient. Egos that are quick to anger create excessive pain and suffering for themselves and others. Refer back to Chapter 8 on Rules and Chapter 9 on Ego. You may want to take an anger management course or practice meditation. Get into the habit of counting to ten before saying anything in anger. You may want to memorize and practice the serenity prayer. Developing self-awareness and self-control are necessary to overcome anger and wrath.

KINDNESS VS. ENVY

Answer these questions as honestly as you can:

- Do you practice love and kindness or are you envious of others?

- If a coworker gets the promotion that you felt you deserved, do you congratulate them with sincerity? Do you complain to your boss that you should have gotten the promotion? Do you spread rumors and lies about them in hopes they get fired? Do you cuss them out, curse your boss out, quit your job and storm out in a huff?

- If your friend gets many more compliments from others than do you, do you recognize their beauty and talents and give them sincere compliments as well? Or do you ask for, fish for, or compete with them for those compliments? Do you become passive/aggressive, giving them compliments with veiled insults. Do you go behind their back and tell others why they are undeserving of their compliments?

- Your long-time friend achieves a measure of success and happiness. Do you feel genuinely happy for them and their success and congratulate them? Or do you lie to them about your own success and happiness? Do you feel jealous of their success, and talk ill of them behind their back? Do you abandon the friendship, and work against them in an attempt to diminish their happiness?

Answering **YES** to anything other than the first question is a sign that you need to practice more love and kindness. Refer back to Chapter 6 on Happiness. Acts of genuine love and kindness are the cause of true happiness. We can never gain happiness by taking it from someone else. Happiness is gained through giving only. Give and you will receive. Work at being less selfish and more giving. Use the Observer within to recognize when you are being selfish and self-centered. Then practice being kind, thoughtful and generous.

DILIGENCE VS. SLOTH

Answer these questions as honestly as you can:

- Do you make a list of things to accomplish each day? Or do you plan to do as little as possible each day? Do you pick up the dirty clothes on the floor and put it in the laundry? Or are you more likely to kick it under the bed?

- Do you take your dog for a nice long walk? Or are you more likely to put your dog on a chain in the back yard? Do you work until the job is done? Or do you try to get home as early as possible? Do you prefer to play sports? Or do you prefer to watch them on TV? Do you clean up after yourself? Or do you ignore it and wait for someone else to do it? Do you make a plan on how to get rich? Or are you just hoping to win the lottery? Do you usually make your bed every day? Or do you almost never make your bed?

- Do you go to work regularly? Or do you collect unemployment and food stamps? Do you persist even in the face of adversity? Or do you give up at the first sign of defeat?

Answering the **OR** questions suggest that you need to work on becoming less lazy. Making genuine progress in our spiritual growth and evolution requires hard work. Refer to Chapter 12 on Work. If we are naturally lazy, progress will be slow indeed. Sloth is one of the most difficult tendencies to overcome. If we don't like work of any kind, work on ourselves won't come easy. Diligence or persistence is the key to success in any endeavor. The persistent desire to be a better person is essential for our continued spiritual growth and evolution. If you tend to be lazy and unproductive and want to change, then I suggest getting into the habit of making lists. This is a habit of successful productive people. Your first list should be of your vices. As you go through this self-evaluation, make a list of the areas of your character that are in need of improvement. We can't fix or change something we don't see. Once the list is made, tackle one at a time. You are then on the road to self-improvement, spiritual growth and evolution.

CHARITY VS. GREED

Answer these questions as honestly as you can:

- Are you selfish or selfless? Are you greedy or charitable? Are you cheap or generous? If you pass a homeless person in the street, do you give them a few bucks? Or are you more likely to avoid eye contact and keep walking?

- If you find a purse or wallet, do you attempt to track down the owner and return it? Or are you more likely to keep the cash and toss the evidence?

- When you receive mail from a charity, do you fill it out and give what you can afford? Or do you toss it in the trash without opening it? When a relative or friend asks you for a loan, do you work out an equitable arrangement? Or do you lie and tell them you are broke?

- When your teenage children ask for money, do you give it to them without thought of repayment? Or do you lend it to them, keep a written record and enforce repayment?

When you get the bill in a restaurant, do you generally tip 15% or more? Or do you tip less than 15% or not at all?

If you answered **YES** to the questions beginning with **OR**, you might be on the stingy side. Refer back to Chapters 6 and 8 on Rules and Happiness. True happiness is found through giving abundantly. We cannot give without receiving, it's the law of the universe. Some of the richest people on earth have attempted to give away their fortunes, only to discover that whatever they give away comes right back to them. One of the reasons we are here on earth is to learn how to give abundantly, like our Heavenly Father. Be perfect as He is perfect. Do you want to experience abundance? Give abundantly! Do you want to experience true and lasting happiness? Give abundantly! If you have much and give much, more will be given to you. If you have little and keep it to yourself, even the little you have will be taken from you.

TEMPERANCE VS. GLUTTONY

Answer these questions as honestly as you can:

- If you drink alcohol, do you drink to be sociable? Or do you drink to get drunk? When you eat a meal, do you eat until you are satisfied? Or do you eat until the plate is empty? When you eat at a buffet, do you stop eating when you are satisfied? Or do you stop eating only when you couldn't possibly eat any more?

- If you smoke cigarettes, do you smoke less than a pack a day? Or do you smoke one after another all day long? If you do recreational drugs, do you do them occasionally? Or do you get high all day every day? Do you prefer to have sex three times a week? Or perhaps three times a day?

- Answering **YES** to the **OR** questions suggest that you may have an addictive personality. Refer back to Chapter 8 on Rules and Chapter 3 on Duality, and Chapter 9 on Ego.

Addictions are synonymous with gluttony. Gluttony is the epitome of selfishness. We cannot achieve happiness through selfish overindulgence. The work involved in overcoming self-indulgences is the practice of temperance or self-control. No progress can be made spiritually until we stop being selfish, and start practicing self-control and generosity. Taking is bad, receiving is good, and giving is better.

CHASTITY VS. LUST

Answer these questions as honestly as you can:

- If you are a teenager, are you putting off sex until you get married? Or are you having sex whenever possible? If you are a young adult, are you looking for a life partner? Or are you looking for a temporary sexual partner? If you are married, do you have sex only with your spouse? Or do you have sex with anyone you can?

- If you are a man, do you think of having sex only with your wife? Or do you think about having sex with every attractive woman you meet?

- Do you prefer to watch a romantic comedy? Or do you watch porn instead?

If you answered **YES** to the **OR** questions, you may need to do some work on curbing your lustful nature. Refer back to the Chapter 8 on Rules and Chapter 6 on Happiness, and Chapter 3 on Duality.

The desire to have sex, and procreate is a natural human emotion, instilled in us by God. It's an imperative that ensures the survival of our species. However, we must not allow ourselves to fall prey to lustful desires. We should not desire sex for the sake of sex. Lust is a selfish desire. It causes us to "take" pleasure from others. This is detrimental to our spiritual growth and evolution. Lustful tendencies increase our negative Karmic Quotient and increase our Karmic debt. This path leads to intense suffering. "Players" run the risk of incurring huge Karmic penalties. Especially married people who have affairs with other married people. This is the surest way to create tremendous pain and suffering in this lifetime and the next. This requires work on self-control. If we use the Observer to catch ourselves thinking lustful thoughts and desires, and then just remind ourselves to stop, change the subject as it were, we can break this habit with practice.

All of us are unique. We each have our own unique blend of virtues and vices. Sometimes we are virtuous, other times we are vicious. Walking the spiritual path means getting to know yourself, intimately. We have to bring awareness to our actions and reactions, so we can perceive our strengths and weaknesses. Consciously molding our own character by instilling virtuous habits and weeding out our vices is the righteous path to God. We start down this path once we desire within our hearts to become a better human being.

Desire is a start, but it's not nearly enough. What's needed is work—lots of work. Finding the Omnipresent Lord within does not mean that life will be full of sunshine and rainbows. God still requires us to work our way out of this world of illusions. We still have to work to provide for our families and communities. God expects us to utilize all the gifts, talents and opportunities he provides for us to make our way in the world. There is an old Buddhist saying that goes, "Before enlightenment, chop wood, carry water, after enlightenment, chop wood, carry water."

Recognizing illusions and then overcoming them is a process. It happens over a long period of time. As a matter of fact, it never really ends. We are always and in all ways growing and evolving towards our inevitable perfection. Embracing this process will ensure a life filled with peace, love and true and lasting happiness.

May God bless you on your Quest!

THE SERVICE BODY

After much hard work, self-control, self-correction and self-less service to others, we are then eligible to receive the ultimate gift from our Heavenly Father. What is the ultimate spiritual gift? It is a service body. What is a service body? It is a physical body that has been blessed and sanctified by the Lord. A perfected human is a useful tool in the hands of the Lord. A tool He wields to the benefit all of mankind. A person with a service body is now an agent of the Lord. He is now a vessel through which the power of God flows out to all humanity. The work he now does is not his own. His work is God's work. His labors are no longer difficult but rather effortless, joyful and fulfilling. "For my yoke is easy and my burden is light." (Matthew 11:30) He lives in a constant state of Peace, Love and Happiness. The troubles of the world touch him not. Wherever he goes, the Lord goes with him. The Lord uses him to spread divine wisdom and Truth, heal the sick, perform miracles and change the world for the better.

Until we are gifted with a service body, it is our responsibility to find good works to engage in. We have to seek out those in need and provide for them in some way. We have to be ever-vigilant in our desire to serve others. Once we are gifted with a service body, that responsibility vanishes. Our only responsibility is to be ever-ready to respond to the commands of the Lord within. We are on call twenty-four seven. Without any forewarning or notice, the Lord can take over our bodies, possess us as it were. He works through us to do His will upon the earth. The work we do is His work. We maintain a passive role, only witnessing what is transpiring. To others in attendance, from their perspective, it is we who are acting, for they have no idea that we are not in control of our actions. They are not aware that we are being guided solely by the hand of the Lord.

Jesus himself performed no miracles. Rather it was in the indwelling Spirit of God that fulfilled his desires in a miraculous fashion. More accurately, the Lord within was quick to manifest Jesus' selfless desires by working through His service body. When Jesus spoke to the masses, it was His Father speaking through Him. "I do nothing on my own, but speak just what the Father has taught me." (John 8:28) "The Son can do nothing of himself, but what he sees the Father do, whatever the Father does, the son also does." (John 5:19) "Don't you believe that I am in the Father and the Father is in me? The words I say to you are not just my own. Rather it is the Father, living in me who *does the work.*" (John 14:10)

"By myself I can do nothing." (John 5:30)

Jesus is not the only son of God. We are all sons and daughters of God.

"You are all sons of God through faith in Christ Jesus." (Galatians 3:26) "Because those who are led by the Spirit of God, are sons of God." (Romans 8:14) "That all of them may be one Father, just as you are in me and I am in you." (John 17:21) "Is it not written that ye are Gods?" (John 10:34) "Behold, what manner of Love the Father has bestowed upon us, that we should be called the sons of God." (John 3:1)

As sons and daughters of God, we too are capable of perfection and of performing miracles. "Be ye perfect as your Heavenly Father is perfect." (Matthew 5:48) "I tell you the truth, anyone who has faith in me will do what I have been doing, and even greater things than these." (John 14:12) "With God all things are possible." (Matthew 19:26)

God our Father is Omnipresent. His awareness is all-pervasive. He is right here, right now. We can communicate with him directly, for he exists within our very own minds. Nor will people say, "here it is" or "there it is", because the kingdom of God is within you. (Luke 17:21) "Are not two sparrows sold for a penny? Yet not one of them will fall to ground apart from the will of your Father." (Matthew 10:29) "Jesus, *knowing all* that was going to happen to him, went out ..." (John 18:4)

Work is never-ending. At all times we should be working on our own character, working on changing our bad habits into good habits, working on understanding Truth and /or working for the benefit of our fellow man. This is the spiritual Path to Enlightenment. This is the Path to God Realization. This is the path to true and lasting happiness.

May the Lord bless you on your Quest to realizing true and lasting happiness in your life!

God, our Heavenly Father, The Creator of All, the Source of all Love, Light and Life,

Omnipresent, Omnipotent and Omniscient, exists within each of us, even while in

Duality consciousness. Our senses may perceive separateness, however, this is but an

Illusion. We can never be separated from our true Source. To perceive Him we need to

Surrender to His will, knowing He loves us, guides us and protects us. True and lasting

Happiness is ours once we succeed in surrendering unto Him, Spiritual growth and

Evolution unfold rapidly. He guides us down the Path of Righteousness, teaching us the

Rules of the road. He teaches us how to live within His Universal Laws. We see our

Ego and how it is the only thing standing between us and Him. Truth is, God is here

Now. We are His children, made in His image and likeness. We are eternal souls, the

Observer within. Pure consciousness, to experience these Truths, we need to

Work on ourselves, giving abundantly, loving unconditionally, and forgiving everything.

BIBLIOGRAPHY

Achad, Frater. "**Ancient Mystical White Brotherhood.**" Great Seal Press. 1971.

Arnold, Edwin. "**The Light of Asia.**" The Theosophical Company. 1998.

Barnard, George. "**In the service of 11:11.**" 11:11 Publishers. 2004.

Beasant, Annie and Charles W. Leadbeater. "**Thought-Forms.**" The Theosophical Publishing House. 1901.

Beck, Lilla and Philippa Pullar. "**Healing with Chakra Energy.**" Destiny Books. 1995.

Blanchard, Ken and Barbara Glanz. "**The Simple Truths of Service.**" Blanchard Family Partnerships. 2005.

Blavatsky, Madame H. P. "**The Secret Doctrine: The Synthesis of Science, Religion and Philosophy.**" The Theosophical Company. 1888.

Bruce, Robert. "**Astral Dynamics.**" Hampton Roads. 1999.

Castaneda, Carlos. "**A Separate Reality.**" Washington Square Press. 1971.

Castaneda, Carlos. "**Tales of Power.**" Washington Square Press. 1974.

Castaneda, Carlos. "**The Active Side of Infinity.**" Harper Perennial. 1998.

Castaneda, Carlos. "**The Art of Dreaming.**" Harper Perennial. 1993

Castaneda, Carlos. "**The Eagles Gift.**" Washington Square Press. 1981.

Castaneda, Carlos. "**The Fire from Within.**" Washington Square Press. 1984.

Castaneda, Carlos. "**The Second Ring of Power.**" Washington Square Press. 1977.

Castaneda, Carlos. "**The Teachings of Don Juan.**" Washington Square Press. 1968.

Castaneda, Carlos. "**The Wheel of Time.**" Washington Square Press. 1998.

Casteneda, Carlos. "**Journey to Ixitlan.**" Washington Square Press. 1972.

Casteneda, Carlos. "**The Power of Silence.**" Washington Square Press. 1987.

Chinmayananda, Swami. "**Narada Bhakti Sutra.**" Central Chinmaya Mission Trust. 1990.

Dali Lama, "**The Art of Happiness.**" Riverhead Books. 1998.

Darwin, Charles. "**The Origin of Species.**" Originally published in London by J Murray. 1859.

Davis, Dr. Charles. "**Spirit Speaks.**" The Church of Metaphysical Christianity. 1988.

Drosnin, Michael. "**The Bible Code.**" Simon and Schuster. 1997.

Eagle Feather, Ken. "**On the Toltec Path.**" Bear and Company. 1995.

Fremantle, Francesca. "**The Tibetan Book of the Dead.**" Shambhala Press. 1992.

Frissell, Bob. "**You are a Spiritual Being Having a Human Experience.**" Frog, Limited. 2001.

Georgian, Linda. "**Your Guardian Angels.**" Fireside, Simon and Schuster. 1994.

Gilchrist, Cherry. "**Theosophy: The Wisdom of the Ages.**" Harper, San Fransisco. 1988.

Gomes, Michael. "**Isis Unveiled by Helena Blavatsky.**" Quest Books. 1997.

Hall, Manly P. "**The Secret Teachings of all Ages.**" Penguin Group. 2003.

Harris, Barbara. "**Conversations with Mary.**" Heron House Publishers. 1999.

Hicks, Esther and Jerry. "**Money, and the Law of Attraction.**" Hay House Publishing. 2008.

Hieromonk, Damascene. "**Christ the Eternal Tao.**" Valaam Books. 1999.

Hurtak, J.J. "**Pistis Sophia.**" The Academy of Future Science. 1999.

Hurtak, J.J. "**The Keys of Enoch.**" The Academy of Future Science. 1977.

Johari, Harish. "**Chakras: Energy Centers of Transformation.**" Destiny Books. 1987.

Jones, Marie, and Larry Flaxman. "**11:11 The Time Prompt Phenomenon.**" The Career Press Inc. 2009.

Judge, William Q. "**Echoes from the Orient.**" The Theosophical Company. 1890.

Judge, William Q. "**Notes on the Bavagad Gita.**" The Theosophical Company. 1918.

Judge, William Q. "**Patanjali's Yoga Aphorisms.**" The Theosophical Company. 1987.

Judge, William Q. **"The Dhammapada."** The Theosophical Company. 1918.

Judge, William Q. **"Vernal Blooms."** The Theosophical Company. 1946.

Kirkwood, Annie. **"Mary's Message to the World."** G.P. Putnam's Sons. 1991.

Krishnamurti, J. **"At the Feet of the Master."** Yogi Publication Society. ISBN# 0-911662-17-0. 2005.

Leadbeater, C.W. **"The Chakras."** The Theosophical Publishing House. 1927.

Leadbeater,C.W. **"The Masters and the Path."** The Theosophical Publishing House. 1925.

Melchizedek, Drunvalo. **"The Ancient Secret of the Flower of Life."** Volumes 1, 2 and 3. Light Technology Publishing. 1990.

Men's Devotional Bible, New International Version. Zondervan Publishing House. 1993.

Meyer, Marvin W. **"The Secret Teachings of Jesus."** Vitage Books. 1986.

Millman, Dan. **"Bridge Between Worlds."** H. J. Kramer. 1999.

Millman, Dan. **"Way of the Peaceful Warrior."** H.J. Kramer. 1980.

Mitchell, Stephen. **" Tao Te Ching by Lao Tzu."** Frances Lincoln Limited. 1999.

Monroe, Robert A. **"Ultimate Journey."** Broadway Books. 1994.

Moore, Thomas. **"Soulmates."** Harper Perennial. 1994.

Muir, Charles and Caroline. **"Tantra, The Art of Conscious Loving."** Mercury House. 1989.

Mumford, Dr. John. **"A Chakra and Kundalini Workbook."** Llewellyn Publications. 1997.

Narby, Jeremy. **"The Cosmic Serpent: DNA and the origins of Knowledge."** Tarcher Penguin. 1998.

Paramahansa, Yogananda. **"A World in Transition."** Self-Realization Fellowship. 1999.

Paulsen, Norman. **"The Christ Consciousness: The Pure Self Within You."** The Builders Publishing Company. 1980.

Paulson, Genevieve. **"Kundalini and the Chakras."** Llewellyn Publications. 2003.

Pinkham, Mark. **"The Return of The Serpents of Wisdom."** Adventures Unlimited Press. 1997.

Russell, Walter. **"The Secret of Light."** University of Science and Philosophy. 1947.

Sannella, Lee, M.D. "**The Kundalini Experience.**" Integral Publishing. 1987.

Schucman, Helen. "**A Course in Miracles.**" Penguin Group. 1996.

Sheng-ye, Ch'an Master. "**Complete Enlightenment.**" Shambhala. 1997.

Smith, Huston. "**World's Religions: A Guide to our Wisdom Traditions.**" Harper, San Francisco. !986.

Solara. "**11:11 Inside the Doorway.**" Star-borne Unlimited. 1992.

Spalding, Baird T. "**Life and Teachings of the Masters of the Far East.**" Vol. 1-6. Devorss and Company. 1924.

Tolle, Eckhart. "**A New Earth: Awakening to Your Life's Purpose.**" Plume, Penquin Group. 2005.

Tolle, Eckhart. "**The Power of Now.**" Namaste Publishing. 1999.

Too, Lillian. "**Chinese Wisdom.**" Freidman/Fairfax Publishers. 2001.

Walsh, Neal Donald. "**Friendship with God.**" G.P. Putnam's Sons. 2003.

Walsh, Neale Donald. "**Conversations with God.**" G.P. Putnum's Sons. 1998.

Wasserman, James. "**The Mystery Traditions: Sacred Symbols and Sacred Art.**" Destiny Books. 1993.

Waxman, Bob. "**Kabbalah Simply Stated.**" Paragon House. 2004.

Webster, Richard. "**Astral Travel for Beginners.**" Llewellyn Publications. 1998.

Yogananda, Paramahansa. "**Autobiography of a Yogi.**" Self-Realization Fellowship. 1946.

Yogananda, Paramahansa. "**Man's Eternal Quest.**" Self-Realization Fellowship. 1975.

Yogananda, Paramahansa. "**The Bavagad Gita.**" Self-Realization Fellowship. 1995.

Yogananda, Paramahansa. "**The Second Coming of Christ.**" Self-Realization Fellowship. 2004.

Zukav, Gary. "**Soul Stories.**" Simon and Schuster. 2000.

Zukav, Gary. "**The Dancing Wu Li Masters; An Overview of New Physics.**" Bantam New Age Books. 1979.

A NOTE FROM THE AUTHOR

Thank you for reading my book, I am sincerely honored. I hope you found it informative and thought provoking. If this philosophy resonates with you, and you would like to see more people embracing these Truths, then please help me to spread these teachings. To start, give this copy to someone you think would benefit from it. You can go to Amazon.com, bring up the page for this book and write a quick review, this will go a long way to helping the book surface on the web site. You can spread the word through social media, and friend me on Facebook. You can start a study group in your area. You can donate copies to your local drug and alcohol rehab facility, crisis center, jail or homeless center. If you wish to send a cash donation, all money received will go towards the dissemination of these materials. If this book helped you to find the Lord within, please write to me and share your story, as I may use it in my next book. I am also available for speaking engagements.

Please send all inquiries and donations to:

The Mitreya Center
5318 34th St East
Bradenton, Florida 34203

If you live in the Sarasota/Bradenton area, and would like to discuss these teachings further, please join us for one or more of our study groups. We welcome all sincere seekers of Truth regardless of their religious affiliations. We also welcome those seeking an understanding of God for the first time in their lives.

For an event and class schedule,
contact Gopi or Neela Chari at 941-751-6950.

CPSIA information can be obtained at www.ICGtesting.com
Printed in the USA
BVOW032249031012

302037BV00006B/142/P

9 781614 931010